Super

Awesome

Casserole

Recipes

About the Author

Laura Sommers is **The Recipe Lady!**

She is the #1 Best Selling Author of over 80 recipe books.

She is a loving wife and mother who lives on a small farm in Baltimore County, Maryland and has a passion for all things domestic especially when it comes to saving money. She has a profitable eBay business and is a couponing addict, avid blogger and YouTuber.

Follow her tips and tricks to learn how to make delicious meals on a budget, save money or to learn the latest life hack!

Visit her blog for even more great recipes and to learn which books are **FREE** for download each week:

http://the-recipe-lady.blogspot.com/

Visit her Amazon Author Page to see her latest books:

amazon.com/author/laurasommers

Laura Sommers is also an Extreme Couponer and Penny Hauler! If you would like to find out how to get things for **FREE** with coupons or how to get things for only a **PENNY**, then visit her couponing blog **Penny Items and Freebies**

http://penny-items-and-freebies.blogspot.com/

© Copyright 2016. Laura Sommers.
All rights reserved.
No part of this book may be reproduced in any form or by any electronic or
mechanical means without written permission of the author. All text, illustrations
and design are the exclusive property of
Laura Sommers

About the Author ii

Introduction 1

Chicken Florentine Casserole...2

Chicken Enchilada Casserole 3

Swiss Chicken Casserole...4

Chicken Cordon Bleu Casserole 4

Chicken and Biscuit Casserole..5

King Ranch Chicken Casserole 6

Cashew Chicken Casserole 7

Almond Chicken Casserole..7

Pesto Chicken Penne Casserole 8

Chicken Taco Casserole..9

Buffalo Chicken Casserole...10

Chicken and Potato Casserole 11

Poppy Seed Chicken Casserole 12

Chicken and Black Bean Casserole 12

Spicy Southwest Chicken Casserole 13

Spicy Tomato Chicken Casserole 14

Chicken Celery Casserole 15

Chicken and Green Bean Casserole 15

Chicken, Stuffing and Green Bean Casserole 16

Chicken and Stuffing Casserole 17

Chicken and Rice Casserole 17

Curried Chicken and Brown Rice Casserole 18

Curried Chicken with Mango Rice 18

Chicken Avocado Casserole 19

Broccoli Chicken Casserole 20

Chicken Wellington Casserole 21

Chicken Reuben Casserole...21

Chicken and Chinese Noodles Casserole 22

Chicken Alfredo Quinoa Casserole 23

Chicken Zucchini Rice Casserole 24

Chicken and Noodle Casserole 25

Dill Chicken Casserole 25

Potato Chip Chicken Casserole...26

Chicken Casserole Del Sol..26

Tuna Casserole 27

Tuna Stroganoff Casserole 28

Tuna Cashew Casserole..28

Spinach Tuna Casserole 29

Tuna Rice Puff Casserole..30

Tomato Tuna Casserole 31

Cheese Lover's Tuna Casserole..31

Tuna Garden Casserole...32

Curry Tuna and Rice Casserole...33

Portuguese Tuna Rice Casserole..34

Tuna Noodle Asparagus Casserole...35

Mushroom Tuna Noodle Casserole..35

Tater Tot Casserole 36

Chili Rellenos Casserole 37

Chili Dog Casserole 38

Corn Dog Casserole 38

Baked Corn Casserole...39

Cheesy Corn Casserole...40

Mexican Beef and Corn Casserole 40

Chili Beef Casserole 41

Beef Nacho Casserole 42

Barbeque Beef Casserole...42

Beef Potato House Pie Casserole...43

Potato Pizza Casserole...44

Hamburger Potato Casserole...45

Pork Chop and Potato Casserole 45

Hamburger Potato Casserole...46

Ham and Potato Casserole...46

Ham, Potato and Broccoli Casserole 47

Ham and Swiss Casserole..48

Ham and Noodle Casserole..48

Pierogi Casserole...49

Pineapple Casserole..50

Bean Casserole 51

Spinach and Bean Casserole...52

Oyster Casserole 52

Mediterranean Casserole 53

Italian Casserole 53

Meatball Sandwich Casserole..54

Lentil Casserole 55

Cauliflower Casserole 56

Sauerkraut Casserole 56

Crab Casserole...57

Shrimp and Crab Casserole...58

Baked Spaghetti Casserole..58

Cowboy Casserole...59

Chow Mein Noodle Casserole..60

Reuben Casserole 61

Sloppy Joe Casserole...61

Frito Casserole...62

Chickpea Casserole..63

Philly Cheesesteak Casserole 64

Eggs and Bacon Casserole..65

Vegetarian Chili Casserole..65

Sweet Potato Casserole 66

Sweet Potato and Apple Casserole 67

Sweet Potato Pineapple Casserole 67

Yellow Squash Casserole 68

Zucchini Cornbread Casserole 69

Broccoli Casserole 69

Green Bean Casserole..70

Pulled Pork Casserole..70

Spinach Casserole..71

Potato and Egg Casserole 72

Green Chile Egg Casserole..72

Sausage Egg Casserole 73

Spinach and Mushroom Egg Casserole 74

Raisin Bread French Toast Casserole 74

Pear and Almond French Toast Casserole.......................................75

Blueberry French Toast Casserole..76

Mexican Turkey Corn Bread Casserole 77

Turkey and Hash Brown Casserole....................................78

Turkey Butternut Squash Casserole 79

Pancake and bacon Casserole 80

Pancake and Sausage Casserole 81

Bacon Waffle Casserole 82

Lobster Mac and Cheese Casserole....................................83

Pumpkin Casserole....................................85

Pumpkin Breakfast Casserole 86

Cheesy Zucchini Casserole 87

Cheesy Sausage Zucchini Casserole....................................88

About the Author 89

Other books by Laura Sommers....................................90

Introduction

Casseroles are not just for leftovers. Casseroles are an easy way to prepare a quick and economical meal for the family. Casseroles are great for breakfast, lunch or dinner. Perfect for the weekend or week night. When you have a lot of mouths to feed, whether it is a party or just a large family, casseroles are a crowd pleaser that doesn't break the bank.

Chicken Florentine Casserole

Ingredients:

4 skinless, boneless chicken breast halves
1/4 cup butter
3 tsps. minced garlic
1 tbsp. lemon juice
1 (10.75 oz.) can condensed cream of mushroom soup
1 tbsp. Italian seasoning
1/2 cup half-and-half
1/2 cup grated Parmesan cheese
2 (13.5 oz.) cans spinach, drained
4 oz. fresh mushrooms, sliced
2/3 cup bacon bits

Directions:

1. Preheat oven to 350 degrees F (175 degrees C).
2. Place the chicken breast halves on a baking sheet; bake 20 to 30 minutes, until no longer pink and juices run clear. Remove from heat, and set aside.
3. Increase the oven temperature to 400 degrees F (200 degrees C).
4. Melt the butter in a medium saucepan over medium heat.
5. Stirring constantly, mix in the garlic, lemon juice, cream of mushroom soup, Italian seasoning, half-and-half, and Parmesan cheese.
6. Arrange the spinach over the bottom of a 9x9 inch baking dish.
7. Cover the spinach with the mushrooms.
8. Pour half the mixture from the saucepan over the mushrooms.
9. Arrange chicken breasts in the dish, and cover with the remaining sauce mixture.
10. Sprinkle with bacon bits, and top with mozzarella cheese.
11. Bake 20 to 25 minutes in the 400 degrees F (200 degrees C) oven, until bubbly and lightly browned.

Chicken Enchilada Casserole

Ingredients:

6 tbsps. butter, divided
6 skinless, boneless chicken breast halves
2 fresh poblano peppers, seeded and sliced into strips
4 fresh jalapeno peppers, seeded and diced
2 cloves garlic, chopped
1 lime, halved
1/4 cup all-purpose flour
1 pint half-and-half
1 bunch fresh cilantro, chopped
1 (8 oz.) pkg. fresh mushrooms, sliced
2 oz. sour cream
12 (6 inch) corn tortillas

Directions:

1. Melt 2 tbsps. butter in a large skillet over medium heat.
2. Place the chicken breasts in the skillet.
3. Mix in the poblano peppers, jalapeno peppers, and garlic.
4. Squeeze the juice from one lime half over the chicken, and place the lime peel and pulp into the skillet.
5. Cover, and simmer 25 minutes, stirring occasionally, until chicken juices run clear.
6. Remove from heat, cool, and cut chicken into cubes.
7. Preheat oven to 350 degrees F (175 degrees C).
8. Melt 1/4 cup butter in a medium saucepan over low heat.
9. Gradually stir in the flour and half-and-half.
10. Mix in the cilantro, mushrooms, sour cream, and juice of remaining lime half.
11. Cook and stir 10 minutes, until mushrooms are tender.
12. Line the bottom of a 9x13 inch baking dish with 6 tortillas.
13. Arrange 1/2 the chicken and pepper mixture over the tortillas.
14. Sprinkle with 1 cup cheese, and cover with remaining tortillas.
15. Layer with remaining chicken and pepper mixture, and pour the cilantro sauce evenly over the casserole. Top with remaining cheese.
16. Bake 25 minutes, until cheese is melted and lightly browned.

Swiss Chicken Casserole

Ingredients:

6 skinless, boneless chicken breasts
6 slices Swiss cheese
1 (10.75 oz.) can condensed cream of chicken soup
1/4 cup milk
2 cups herb-seasoned stuffing mix
1/4 cup butter

Directions:

1. Preheat oven to 350 degrees F (175 degrees C).
2. Arrange chicken in a greased 12 x 8 x 2 baking dish.
3. Top with Swiss cheese slices.
4. Combine soup and milk and stir well.
5. Spoon mixture over chicken and sprinkle with stuffing mix.
6. Drizzle butter or margarine over crumbs.
7. Cover and bake at 350 degrees F (175 degrees C) for 50 minutes.
8. Enjoy!

Chicken Cordon Bleu Casserole

Ingredients:

1 egg
1/2 cup milk
2 lbs. skinless, boneless chicken breast halves, cut into chunks
1 cup plain dried bread crumbs
1 cup oil for frying
8 oz. Swiss cheese, cubed
8 oz. cubed ham
1 (10.75 oz.) can condensed cream of chicken soup
1 cup milk

Directions:

1. Preheat oven to 350 degrees F (175 degrees C).
2. Beat egg and 1/2 cup milk together until combined.
3. Stir in the chicken chunks to coat, then drain, and coat with bread crumbs.
4. Heat oil in a large skillet to 375 degrees F (190 degrees C).
5. Fry breaded chicken cubes in hot oil until golden brown on all sides, then remove, and drain on paper towels.
6. Place chicken cubes in a glass baking dish, along with the Swiss cheese, and ham.
7. Stir together the soup with 1 cup milk, pour over casserole.
8. Bake until golden brown and bubbly, about 30 minutes.

Chicken and Biscuit Casserole

Ingredients:

1/4 cup butter
2 cloves garlic, minced
1/2 cup chopped onion
1/2 cup chopped celery
1/2 cup chopped baby carrots
1/2 cup all-purpose flour
2 tsps. white sugar
1 tsp. salt
1 tsp. dried basil
1/2 tsp. ground black pepper
4 cups chicken broth
1 (10 oz.) can peas, drained
4 cups diced, cooked chicken meat
2 cups buttermilk baking mix
2 tsps. dried basil
2/3 cup milk

Directions:

1. Preheat oven to 350 degrees F (175 degrees C).
2. Lightly grease a 9x13 inch baking dish.
3. In a skillet, melt the butter over medium-high heat.
4. Cook and stir the garlic, onion, celery, and carrots in butter until tender. Mix in the flour, sugar, salt, 1 tsp. dried basil, and pepper.
5. Stir in broth, and bring to a boil.
6. Stirring constantly, boil 1 minute, reduce heat, and stir in peas. Simmer 5 minutes, then mix in chicken.
7. Transfer mixture to the prepared baking dish.
8. In a medium bowl, combine the baking mix and 2 tsps. dried basil.
9. Stir in milk to form a dough. Divide the dough into 6 to 8 balls.
10. On floured wax paper, use the palm of your hand to flatten each ball of dough into a circular shape; place on top of chicken mixture.
11. Bake for 30 minutes. Cover with foil, and bake for 10 more minutes.
12. To serve, spoon chicken mixture over biscuits.

King Ranch Chicken Casserole

Ingredients:

1 (3 lb.) chicken, boiled and deboned
1 (14.5 oz.) pkg. tortilla chips
1 (10 oz.) can diced tomatoes with green chile peppers
1 (10.75 oz.) can condensed cream of chicken soup
1 (10.75 oz.) can condensed cream of mushroom soup
1 onion, chopped
3 cups shredded Cheddar cheese

Directions:

1. Preheat oven to 300 degrees F (150 degrees C.)
2. Layer the chips in a 9x13 inch casserole dish.
3. Combine the tomatoes, chicken soup, mushroom soup and onion.
4. Pour half of mixture over chips. Layer the chicken pieces, half of the cheese and the remaining soup mixture.
5. Bake at 300 degrees F (150 degrees C) for 20 minutes.
6. Top with the remaining cheese and return to the oven until the cheese is melted.

Cashew Chicken Casserole

Ingredients:

1 cup chicken broth
1 (10.75 oz.) can condensed cream of chicken soup
1 (10.75 oz.) can condensed cream of mushroom soup
2 tbsps. soy sauce
1 (2 to 3 lb.) whole chicken, cut into pieces
4 cups hot cooked rice
1 cup cashew nuts

Directions:

1. Preheat oven to 400 degrees F (200 degrees C).
2. Combine the broth, cream of chicken soup, mushroom soup and soy sauce in a large saucepan and bring to a boil; add chicken, rice and 3/4 cup cashews.
3. Mix well and pour mixture into a 9x13 inch baking dish.
4. Sprinkle remaining 1/4 cup cashews on top.
5. Bake for 20 to 25 minutes, or until chicken is cooked through and no longer pink inside.

Almond Chicken Casserole

Ingredients:

2 cups uncooked long-grain rice
1/2 tbsp. butter
4 tbsps. chopped onion
2 cups diced celery
3 cups cooked, chopped chicken breast meat
1 cup mayonnaise
1 (10.75 oz.) can condensed cream of chicken soup
1/2 cup blanched slivered almonds
1 cup crushed cornflake crumbs
2 tbsps. butter

Directions:

1. In a saucepan bring water to a boil. Add rice and stir.
2. Reduce heat, cover and simmer for 20 minutes.
3. Set aside.
4. Melt 1/2 tbsp. butter in a medium skillet over medium heat; saute onion and celery until soft.
5. Preheat oven to 350 degrees F (175 degrees C).
6. Combine the chicken, rice, onion and celery in a 9x13 inch baking dish.
7. Stir in mayonnaise and soup, then almonds. Top with crushed cornflakes and 2 tbsps. butter.
8. Bake for 45 minutes, until golden brown.

Pesto Chicken Penne Casserole

Ingredients:

1/2 cup seasoned bread crumbs
1/2 cup grated Parmesan cheese
1 tbsp. olive oil
1 (16 oz.) box penne pasta
6 cups cubed cooked chicken
4 cups shredded Italian cheese blend
3 cups fresh baby spinach
1 (15 oz.) can crushed tomatoes
1 (15 oz.) jar Alfredo sauce
1 (15 oz.) jar pesto sauce
1 1/2 cups milk

Directions:

1. Preheat an oven to 350 degrees F (175 degrees C).
2. Grease a 9x13-inch baking dish.
3. Combine the bread crumbs, Parmesan cheese, and olive oil in a small bowl until evenly moistened; set aside.
4. Fill a large pot with lightly salted water and bring to a rolling boil over high heat.
5. Once the water is boiling, stir in the penne, and return to a boil.
6. Cook the pasta uncovered, stirring occasionally, until the pasta has cooked through, but is still firm to the bite, about 11 minutes.
7. Drain well in a colander set in the sink.
8. Meanwhile, combine the chicken in a bowl with the Italian cheese blend, spinach, tomatoes, alfredo sauce, pesto sauce, and milk.
9. Stir in the pasta once done, and scoop into the prepared baking dish. Top with the bread crumb mixture.
10. Bake until bubbly and golden brown on top, 40 to 45 minutes.

Chicken Taco Casserole

Ingredients:

4 cups shredded, cooked chicken
2 (10.75 oz.) cans condensed cream of chicken soup
1 cup light sour cream
1 (10 oz.) can diced tomatoes and green chiles, undrained
1 (15 oz.) can black beans, rinsed and drained
1 (1 oz.) envelope taco seasoning mix
5 cups coarsely crushed tortilla chips
2 cups shredded Cheddar cheese
Chopped tomato
Sliced green onion
Chopped fresh cilantro leaves

Directions:

1. Heat the oven to 350 degrees F.
2. Lightly grease a 13x9x2-inch baking dish.
3. Stir the chicken, soup, sour cream, tomatoes and green chiles, beans and seasoning mix in a large bowl.
4. Layer half the chicken mixture, 3 cups tortilla chips and half the cheese in the baking dish.
5. Layer with the remaining chicken mixture and tortilla chips.
6. Cover the baking dish.
7. Bake for 30 minutes. Uncover the baking dish.
8. Sprinkle with the remaining cheese.
9. Bake, uncovered, for 10 minutes or until hot and bubbling and the cheese is melted.
10. Sprinkle with the chopped tomato, green onion and cilantro before serving, if desired.

Buffalo Chicken Casserole

Ingredients:

3 cups shredded cooked chicken
2 tbsps. cayenne pepper sauce
1/3 (16 oz.) pkg. rotini pasta, cooked and drained
1 stalk celery, sliced
1 (10.75 oz.) can condensed cream of chicken soup
1/4 cup blue cheese salad dressing
1 cup shredded Monterey Jack cheese

Directions:

1. Heat the oven to 350 degrees F.
2. Lightly grease an 11x8x2-inch baking dish.
3. Stir the chicken and pepper sauce in a large bowl.
4. Stir in the rotini, celery, soup, dressing and 1/2 cup cheese.
5. Spoon the chicken mixture into the baking dish.
6. Sprinkle with the remaining cheese.
7. Bake for 25 minutes or until the chicken mixture is hot and bubbling and the cheese is melted.

Chicken and Potato Casserole

Ingredients:

Vegetable cooking spray
1 (10.75 oz.) can condensed cream of chicken soup
1 cup sour cream
2 cups shredded Cheddar cheese or Colby Jack cheese
1/2 cup milk
1/2 tsp. garlic powder
1/4 tsp. ground black pepper
1 (28 oz.) pkg. frozen hash browns with onions and peppers, thawed
Salt
3 cups shredded cooked chicken
4 slices bacon, cooked and crumbled

Directions:

1. Heat the oven to 375 degrees F.
2. Spray a 13x9x2-inch baking dish with the cooking spray.
3. Stir the soup, sour cream, 1 cup cheese, milk, garlic powder and black pepper in a medium bowl.
4. Spread the potatoes in the baking dish.
5. Season the potatoes with the salt and additional black pepper.
6. Top with the chicken.
7. Spread the soup mixture over the chicken.
8. Cover the baking dish.
9. Bake for 40 minutes or until the potatoes are tender and the mixture is hot and bubbling. Uncover the baking dish.
10. Sprinkle with the remaining cheese.
11. Bake, uncovered, for 5 minutes or until the cheese is melted. Sprinkle with the bacon and chives before serving.

Poppy Seed Chicken Casserole

Ingredients:

4 skinless, boneless chicken breast halves
1/2 cup butter, melted
1 sleeve buttery round crackers, crushed
1 tsp. poppy seeds
1 (8 oz.) container sour cream
1 (10.75 oz.) can condensed cream of chicken soup
2 cups shredded Cheddar cheese

Directions:

1. Place the chicken breasts into a large pot and cover with water.
2. Bring to a boil over high heat, then reduce heat to medium, cover, and simmer until the chicken breasts are no longer pink in the center, about 20 minutes. Drain the water, then shred the chicken.
3. Preheat an oven to 350 degrees F (175 degrees C).
4. Combine the butter, crackers, and poppy seeds in a bowl.
5. Set aside.
6. Blend the sour cream and cream of chicken soup in a bowl.
7. Pour half of the soup mixture into a 9x9-inch baking dish.
8. Add the shredded chicken, then pour the remaining half of the soup mixture on top. Sprinkle with Cheddar cheese, then top with the cracker mixture.
9. Bake until cheese has melted and the sauce is bubbly, 25 to 30 minutes.

Chicken and Black Bean Casserole

Ingredients:

1 (15.25 oz.) can whole kernel corn, drained
1 (15 oz.) can black beans, rinsed and drained
1 cup salsa verde
1/2 tsp. ground cumin
1/2 tsp. ground coriander
1 (22 oz.) pkg. precooked fajita chicken strips
1 1/2 cups shredded Mexican cheese blend
1/2 cup crushed tortilla chips

Directions:

1. Preheat oven to 350 degrees F.
2. In 2-quart casserole dish combine corn, beans, salsa, cumin, and coriander.
3. Stir in fajita chicken strips and 1 cup of the cheese.
4. Bake, uncovered, 35 to 40 minutes or until bubbly.
5. Sprinkle with the remaining 1/2 cup cheese.
6. Bake 3 to 5 minutes or until cheese is melted.
7. Sprinkle with crushed tortilla chips.

Spicy Southwest Chicken Casserole

Ingredients:

1 lb. skinless, boneless chicken breast halves
1/2 cup water, or as needed
1 large onion, chopped
1 rcd bcll pcppcr, chopped
1 (15 oz.) can black beans, partially drained
1 (14 oz.) can whole kernel corn, drained
3/4 cup picante sauce
1 (4 oz.) can chopped green chiles
2 tbsps. chili powder
1 tbsp. ground cumin
4 (8 inch) flour tortillas
1 (10.75 oz.) can condensed fiesta-style nacho cheese soup
1 (14.5 oz.) can diced tomatoes with green chile peppers
1 cup shredded Mexican cheese blend

Directions:

1. Preheat oven to 350 degrees F (175 degrees C).
2. Grease a 9x13-inch baking dish.
3. Bring chicken breasts and water to a boil in a large skillet; cook over medium heat until chicken juices run clear and meat is no longer pink inside, about 10 minutes.
4. Transfer chicken breasts to a large plate, reserving pan juices in skillet, and shred chicken with 2 forks.
5. Cook onion and red bell pepper in reserved drippings over medium heat until onion is translucent, 5 to 8 minutes.
6. Return shredded chicken to skillet. Stir black beans, corn, picante sauce, chopped green chiles, chili powder, and cumin into chicken mixture until thoroughly combined.
7. Bring mixture to a simmer and cook until heated through, about 5 minutes.
8. Pour chicken mixture into prepared baking dish.
9. Arrange flour tortillas in a single layer over chicken mixture.
10. Stir fiesta soup with diced tomatoes and green chiles in a bowl until thoroughly combined; spread soup mixture over tortillas. Top casserole with Mexican cheese blend.
11. Bake until cheese topping has melted and casserole is hot, about 30 minutes. Cool 5 minutes before serving.

Spicy Tomato Chicken Casserole

Ingredients:

1 (10 oz.) can diced tomatoes with green chile peppers
1 (10.75 oz.) can condensed cream of celery soup
1 (10 oz.) pkg. nacho-flavor tortilla chips
4 skinless, boneless, chicken breast halves, cooked
1 lb. processed cheese, sliced

Directions:

1. In a medium bowl combine the tomatoes and soup and mix together. Set aside.
2. In a lightly greased 2 quart microwave-safe casserole dish layer 1/3 of the tortilla chips, 1/2 of the chicken, 1/2 of the tomato/soup mixture and 1/3 of the cheese.
3. Repeat layers, then top with the remaining tortilla chips and cheese.
4. Preheat oven to 400 degrees F (200 degrees C).
5. Cover dish with lid or aluminum foil and bake for 30 minutes.

Chicken Celery Casserole

Ingredients:

1 tbsp. olive oil
1 large onion, sliced into rings
4 cloves garlic, minced
4 boneless, skinless chicken breast halves, cut into bite-sized pieces
2 (10.75 oz.) cans condensed cream of celery soup
1 cup chopped celery
1 (4 oz.) can mushrooms, drained
1 cup chopped carrot
1 pinch poultry seasoning
Salt and pepper to taste

Directions:

1. Heat oil in a large skillet over medium-high heat.
2. Add onion and garlic, and saute for a few minutes until tender.
3. Add chicken pieces, and fry until lightly browned.
4. Transfer the mixture to a 9x13 inch baking dish, and stir in the celery soup, celery, mushrooms, and carrots.
5. Season with poultry seasoning, salt and pepper to taste.
6. Preheat the oven to 300 degrees F (150 degrees C).
7. Cover the dish, and bake for 2 hours.
8. Serve over chicken flavored rice.

Chicken and Green Bean Casserole

Ingredients:

1 tbsp. olive oil
4 skinless, boneless chicken breast halves
2 (14.5 oz.) cans French-style green beans, drained
1 (10.5 oz.) can condensed cream of chicken soup
3/4 cup mayonnaise
1 tsp. garlic powder
1/4 cup grated Parmesan cheese

Directions:

1. Preheat the oven to 350 degrees F (175 degrees C).
2. Heat olive oil in a large skillet over medium-high heat.
3. Quickly brown the chicken breast halves on both sides.
4. Do not cook through.
5. Remove from heat, and set aside.
6. Pour the green beans into a 2 quart casserole dish.
7. Place the chicken on top of the beans.
8. In a small bowl, mix together the cream of chicken soup and mayonnaise.
9. Spread over the top of the chicken and beans.
10. Sprinkle Parmesan cheese over the top.
11. Bake for 35 to 40 minutes, until the chicken is no longer pink, and the cheese is browned.

Chicken, Stuffing and Green Bean Casserole

Ingredients:

2 cups cooked, cubed chicken breast meat
1 (10.75 oz.) can condensed cream of chicken soup
1 (14.5 oz.) can green beans, drained
salt and pepper to taste
1 (12 oz.) pkg. unseasoned dry bread stuffing mix

Directions:

1. In a medium bowl combine the chicken, soup, beans, salt and pepper.
2. Mix well and set aside.
3. Prepare stuffing according to pkg. directions.
4. Preheat oven to 375 degrees F (190 degrees C).
5. Spoon chicken mixture into a 9x13 inch baking dish, top with prepared stuffing and sprinkle with cheese.
6. Bake, covered, for 25 minutes.
7. Remove cover and bake another 5 minutes to brown the cheese.

Chicken and Stuffing Casserole

Ingredients:

1 (3 lb.) whole chicken
8 oz. dry bread stuffing mix
1 (10.75 oz.) can condensed cream of chicken soup
1 (10.75 oz.) can condensed cream of celery soup
1 1/4 cups chicken broth (from boiling the chicken)
1 cup evaporated milk

Directions:

1. Preheat oven to 350 degrees F (175 degrees C).
2. Layer the deboned chicken meat in a lightly greased 9x13 inch baking dish.
3. Sprinkle stuffing mix over the chicken layer.
4. In a large bowl mix together the soups, broth and evaporated milk. Stir well.
5. Pour this mixture over the stuffing mix, making sure it gets to the bottom of the baking dish.
6. Bake for 35 to 45 minutes, until it starts to bubble in the center.

Chicken and Rice Casserole

Ingredients:

1 cup uncooked white rice
1 (1 oz.) pkg. dry onion soup mix
2 (10.75 oz.) cans condensed cream of mushroom soup
1 (4.5 oz.) can sliced mushrooms
1 cup milk

Directions:

1. Preheat oven to 350 degrees F (175 degrees C).
2. In a large bowl mix the rice, dry onion soup mix, cream of mushroom soup, mushroom pieces and milk.
3. Place the chicken pieces in a 9x13 inch baking dish and pour the mushroom mixture over the chicken.
4. Cover and bake for 1 hour.
5. Uncover and bake for 15 more minutes.

Curried Chicken and Brown Rice Casserole

Ingredients:

1 cup water
1 (8 oz.) can stewed tomatoes
3/4 cup quick-cooking brown rice
1/2 cup raisins
1 tbsp. lemon juice
3 tsps. curry powder
1 cube chicken bouillon
1/2 tsp. ground cinnamon
1/4 tsp. salt
2 cloves garlic, minced
1 bay leaf (optional)
3/4 lb. skinless, boneless chicken breast halves, cut into 1 inch pieces

Directions:

1. Preheat oven to 350 degrees F (175 degrees C).
2. In a skillet, stir together water, stewed tomatoes, brown rice, raisins, lemon juice, curry powder, bouillon, ground cinnamon, salt, garlic, and bay leaf.
3. Bring to a boil; then stir in chicken.
4. Transfer mixture to a casserole dish.
5. Cover, and bake for 45 minutes, stirring occasionally, until rice is tender and chicken juices run clear.

Curried Chicken with Mango Rice

Ingredients:

1 tsp. curry powder, or to taste
1/2 tsp. salt
1/4 tsp. black pepper
4 skinless, boneless chicken breast halves
1 cup chicken broth
1/2 cup water
1/2 cup white wine
1 cup long-grain white rice
1 tbsp. brown sugar
1 tbsp. dried parsley
1 cup diced mango

Directions:

1. Combine curry powder, 1/4 tsp. salt, and pepper.
2. Rub mixture into chicken breasts.
3. Set aside.
4. In a large, non-stick skillet, combine chicken broth, water, and wine with rice.
5. Stir in brown sugar, dried parsley, and remaining 1/4 tsp. salt.
6. Stir in mango.
7. Arrange chicken pieces on top of rice, and bring to a boil.
8. Cover, reduce heat to low, and simmer for 20 to 25 minutes.
9. Remove from heat.
10. Let stand, covered, until all liquid is absorbed, about 5 minutes.

Chicken Avocado Casserole

Ingredients:

7 tbsps. butter, divided
1 tbsp. olive oil
8 skinless, boneless chicken breast halves
1/4 cup all-purpose flour
1 cup light cream
1 cup chicken broth
3/4 tsp. kosher salt
1/4 tsp. ground black pepper
1/2 cup grated Parmesan cheese
2 dashes hot pepper sauce
1/2 tsp. dried rosemary, crushed
1/2 tsp. dried basil
3 cups sliced fresh mushrooms
1/4 cup sherry
1/2 cup sliced almonds, toasted
2 avocados

Directions:

1. Preheat the oven to 350 degrees F.
2. Melt one tbsp. of butter in large heavy skillet.
3. Add olive oil and swirl together with the butter.
4. Add chicken and saute until chicken pieces are browned and juices run clear.
5. Turn pieces to brown evenly while sauteing.
6. Place chicken breasts in 9x13 baking dish and set aside.
7. Melt 4 tbsps. of butter until foamy. Stir in flour, and cook for three minutes, stirring constantly. Slowly add cream and chicken broth. Continue stirring and cooking until smooth and thickened.
8. Season sauce with salt, black pepper, Parmesan cheese, hot pepper sauce and herbs. Set aside.
9. Saute mushrooms in remaining two tbsps. of butter.
10. Add sherry and cook until reduced.
11. Place mushrooms over the chicken.
12. Pour the sauce over the chicken and mushrooms.
13. Bake uncovered for 25 minutes, then sprinkle with almonds, and return to oven for 10 minutes.
14. Peel and slice avocados lengthwise and place over chicken before serving.

Broccoli Chicken Casserole

Ingredients:

2 1/2 cups chopped chicken breast meat
1 (10.75 oz.) can condensed cream of mushroom soup
1/2 cup milk
1/2 cup shredded Monterey Jack cheese
1 (10 oz.) pkg. frozen broccoli
1/2 cup chopped green onion
1 tsp. dried basil
1/2 tsp. ground black pepper

Directions:

1. Preheat oven to 350 degrees F (175 degrees C).
2. In a large bowl combine the chicken, soup, milk, cheese, broccoli, green onion, basil and pepper.
3. Mix well and spread mixture into a lightly greased 9x13 inch baking dish.
4. Bake at 350 degrees F (175 degrees C) for 50 minutes, until bubbly.

Chicken Wellington Casserole

Ingredients:

2 tsps. butter
2 skinless, boneless chicken breast halves
1 (3 oz.) pkg. cream cheese, softened
1/2 cup sliced fresh mushrooms
1 tbsp. chopped green onion
1/8 tsp. salt
1 pinch ground black pepper
1 (4 oz.) pkg. refrigerated crescent rolls

Directions:

1. Preheat oven to 350 degrees F (175 degrees C).
2. Melt butter in a skillet over medium heat.
3. Cook and stir chicken until no longer pink in the center and the juices run clear, about 3 to 4 minutes per side.
4. An instant-read thermometer inserted into the center should read at least 165 degrees F (74 degrees C).
5. Set aside to cool until cool enough to handle; cut into chunks.
6. Mix chicken, cream cheese, mushrooms, green onion, salt, and black pepper together in a bowl.
7. Unroll crescent roll dough.
8. Place a portion of the chicken mixture onto the center of each piece of dough and fold the three corners up, forming a pocket.
9. Pinch edges to seal.
10. Bake until golden brown, about 20 minutes.

Chicken Reuben Casserole

Ingredients:

1 1/4 cups water
1 (6 oz.) pkg. quick-cooking stuffing mix
1 (20 oz.) can sauerkraut, drained
1 (16 oz.) pkg. skinless, boneless chicken breast halves, cut into bite-size pieces
8 oz. shredded Swiss cheese
4 oz. shredded Cheddar cheese
1/2 (16 oz.) bottle French salad dressing

Directions:

1. Preheat oven to 350 degrees F (175 degrees C).
2. Bring water to a boil in a saucepan.
3. Stir stuffing mix into the water, place a lid on the saucepan, and remove pan from heat.
4. Let sit until the stuffing is thickened, about 5 minutes.
5. Fluff stuffing with a fork.
6. Mix sauerkraut, chicken, Swiss cheese, and Cheddar cheese together in a large bowl.
7. Stir enough French dressing into the sauerkraut mixture to moisten to your liking; spread into a casserole dish.
8. Spread stuffing over the sauerkraut mixture.
9. Bake until browned along the edges, about 25 minutes.

Chicken and Chinese Noodles Casserole

Ingredients:

cooking spray
1 tbsp. olive oil
1 small onion, diced
1 (10.75 oz.) can low-fat cream of mushroom soup
1 (10.75 oz.) can water
1/4 tsp. garlic salt, or to taste
ground black pepper to taste
1 roasted chicken, bones and skin removed, meat cut into cubes
1 (8.5 oz.) pkg. chow mein noodles
1 (4 oz.) jar pimentos

Directions:

1. Preheat oven to 350 degrees F (175 degrees C).
2. Prepare a casserole dish with cooking spray.
3. Heat olive oil in a saucepan over medium heat.
4. Cook and stir onion in the hot oil until translucent, 5 to 7 minutes.
5. Add soup and water; stir.
6. Season the mixture with garlic salt and pepper.
7. Layer chicken into the bottom of the prepared casserole dish.
8. Top with chow mein noodles and pimentos.
9. Pour the mixture from the saucepan over the layers to cover.
10. Bake in preheated oven until completely heated through, 20 to 30 minutes.

Chicken Alfredo Quinoa Casserole

Ingredients:

1/4 cup sunflower seed oil
1/2 cup chopped onion
2 tbsps. minced garlic
2 cups quinoa 2 tbsps. chicken bouillon
4 cups water
1 1/2 tsps. chopped fresh thyme
1 1/2 tsps. chopped fresh parsley
2 (5 oz.) cans chicken chunks, drained
2 cups Alfredo sauce
1 (10.75 oz.) can cream of chicken soup
1/4 cup butter, cut into small pieces
3/4 cup shredded Italian cheese blend, divided
1 1/2 cups crushed pita chips
1/4 cup shredded Parmesan cheese

Directions:

1. Heat sunflower oil in a skillet over medium heat; cook and stir onion and garlic until onion is slightly tender, about 5 minutes. Add quinoa and chicken bouillon; cook, stirring frequently, until quinoa is toasted, 5 to 8 minutes.
2. Pour water over quinoa mixture and bring to a boil.
3. Cover and reduce heat to medium-low, and simmer for 10 minutes.
4. Stir thyme and parsley into quinoa mixture and simmer until water is absorbed, about 5 minutes.
5. Remove skillet from heat and fluff quinoa with a fork.
6. Preheat oven to 350 degrees F (175 degrees C).
7. Spread quinoa mixture into the bottom of a 9x13-inch baking dish.
8. Sprinkle chicken over quinoa.
9. Spoon Alfredo sauce and cream of chicken soup over chicken layer; top with butter pieces. Sprinkle 1/2 cup Italian cheese blend over entire mixture.
10. Bake for 15 minutes. Stir mixture and flatten with the back of spoon or spatula.
11. Top with pita chips and remaining 1/4 cup Italian cheese blend.
12. Bake until cheese is melted, about 15 minutes. Cool casserole for 5 minutes; top with Parmesan cheese.

Chicken Zucchini Rice Casserole

Ingredients:

2 cups boiling water
1 cup uncooked white rice
2 cubes chicken bouillon
1 tbsp. olive oil
1 cup thinly sliced zucchini
1/2 cup diced celery
1/2 cup diced onion
1 (10.75 oz.) can condensed cream of mushroom soup
1 (10.75 oz.) can condensed cream of mushroom soup with roasted garlic
1 (8 oz.) can sliced water chestnuts, drained
1 cup diced cooked chicken
1/2 cup mayonnaise
1 tsp. lemon juice
1 (3 oz.) can French-fried onions
Fried onions

Directions:

1. Bring water, rice, and chicken bouillon to a boil in a saucepan.
2. Reduce heat to medium-low, cover, and simmer until the rice is tender and liquid is absorbed, 20 to 25 minutes.
3. Preheat oven to 350 degrees F (175 degrees C).
4. Grease a 9x13-inch baking dish.
5. Heat olive oil in a large skillet over medium heat; cook and stir zucchini, celery, and onion in hot oil until tender, about 5 minutes.
6. Stir rice, cream of mushroom soup, cream of mushroom soup with roasted garlic, water chestnuts, chicken, mayonnaise, and lemon juice into vegetable mixture.
7. Transfer mixture to prepared baking dish.
8. Spread -fried onions over rice mixture.
9. Bake until bubbly and lightly browned, 30 to 35 minutes.

Chicken and Noodle Casserole

Ingredients:

2 boneless chicken breast halves, cooked and cubed
1 (16 oz.) pkg. wide egg noodles
1 (15 oz.) can mixed vegetables
1 cup frozen broccoli
1 (10.75 oz.) can condensed cream of potato soup
1 (10.75 oz.) can condensed cream of broccoli soup
1/4 tsp. dried thyme
1 tsp. salt 1 tsp. ground black pepper
1/2 cup milk
2 cups shredded Colby cheese

Directions:

1. Cook noodles according to pkg. directions.
2. Drain.
3. In a 2 quart saucepan, mix cooked chicken, cream of potato soup, cream of broccoli soup, milk, mixed vegetables, broccoli, salt, pepper, and thyme.
4. Cook over medium heat until broccoli is cooked.
5. Mix with egg noodles. Spread into a greased 9 x 13 inch pan.
6. Cover.
7. Bake at 350 degrees F (175 degrees C) for 20 minutes.
8. Cover with Colby cheese, and bake uncovered for an additional 15 minutes.

Dill Chicken Casserole

Ingredients:

4 boneless chicken breast halves, cooked
1 (10.75 oz.) can condensed cream of chicken soup
1/2 cup milk
1/2 tsp. dried dill weed
1/4 cup sliced green olives
1 (10 oz.) pkg. refrigerated biscuit dough

Directions:

1. Preheat oven to 350 degrees F (175 degrees C).
2. Place cooked chicken breasts in a 7x11 inch baking dish.
3. Combine the soup, milk, dill weed and olives.
4. Mix together and pour mixture over chicken.
5. Top each chicken breast with 2 biscuits.
6. Bake for 20 minutes or until biscuits are golden brown.

Potato Chip Chicken Casserole

Ingredients:

2 cups chopped, cooked chicken meat
1 cup cooked white rice
1 (10.75 oz.) can condensed cream of chicken soup
2/3 cup mayonnaise 2 tbsps. grated onion
1/2 cup chopped celery
1 (8 oz.) can sliced water chestnuts
1 tbsp. lemon juice
1/2 cup shredded sharp Cheddar cheese
2 cups crushed potato chips
1/4 cup water salt and pepper to taste

Directions:

1. Preheat oven to 400 degrees F (200 degrees C).
2. In a large bowl combine the chicken, rice, soup, mayonnaise, onion, celery, water chestnuts, lemon juice, water, salt and pepper.
3. Mix well.
4. Spread this mixture into a lightly greased 9x13 inch baking dish. Cover with cheese, then potato chips.
5. Bake for 20 to 25 minutes or until the potato chips are lightly browned.

Chicken Casserole Del Sol

Ingredients:

1 (16 oz.) pkg. uncooked rigatoni pasta
2 skinless, boneless chicken breast halves
2 (10.75 oz.) cans condensed cream of chicken soup
1 cup mayonnaise
2 tsps. lemon juice
1/2 tsp. curry powder
1 (14.5 oz.) can French-style green beans, drained
1 (4 oz.) can sliced mushrooms, drained
1 cup shredded Cheddar cheese
1/4 cup melted butter
1 cup crushed cornflakes cereal
2 tsps. chopped fresh parsley

Directions:

1. Preheat oven to 375 degrees F (190 degrees C).
2. Cook the rigatoni according to pkg. directions until al dente.
3. Meanwhile, in a separate saucepan, boil the chicken breasts until fully cooked.
4. In a large bowl, combine the soup, mayonnaise, lemon juice, curry powder, green beans and mushrooms.
5. Drain and stir in the rigatoni.
6. Cube the cooked chicken breasts and stir this in as well.
7. Transfer this mixture to a large casserole dish.
8. Sprinkle the cheese on top over all.
9. In a medium bowl, combine the butter and the corn flakes and spread this mixture over the cheese.
10. Finally, top off by sprinkling with the parsley.
11. Bake for 20 to 30 minutes, or until the cheese is bubbly.

Tuna Casserole

Ingredients:

1/2 (8 oz.) pkg. egg noodles
1 (10.75 oz.) can condensed cream of mushroom soup
3/4 cup whole milk
1 (6 oz.) can tuna
2 slices processed cheese
1/2 cup crushed potato chips, or as needed

Directions:

1. Bring a large pot of lightly salted water to a boil.
2. Cook egg noodles in the boiling water, stirring occasionally until cooked through but firm to the bite, about 5 minutes.
3. Drain.
4. Preheat oven to 350 degrees F (175 degrees C).
5. Combine mushroom soup, milk, and tuna in a saucepan over medium heat.
6. Cook until well blended and warmed through, about 5 minutes.
7. Pour mixture into a 9x13-inch baking dish; add noodles and mix well.
8. Top noodles with cheese food and sprinkle potato chips over cheese.
9. Bake until casserole is bubbling, 30 to 45 minutes.

Tuna Stroganoff Casserole

Ingredients:

1 (10.75 oz.) can condensed cream of celery soup
1 cup grated Cheddar cheese
3/4 cup milk
1/2 cup sour cream
1/2 cup mayonnaise
1 (7 oz.) can tuna, drained
2 tbsps. chopped parsley
1 tbsp. lemon juice
1/2 tsp. salt
1/2 tsp. ground black pepper
1 lb. cooked pasta
1 1/2 cups bread crumbs, or to taste

Directions:

1. Preheat oven to 350 degrees F (175 degrees C).
2. Combine cream of celery soup, Cheddar cheese, milk, sour cream, mayonnaise, tuna, parsley, lemon juice, salt, and ground black pepper in a 9x5-inch loaf pan; stir until sauce is well mixed.
3. Toss the pasta into the sauce until thoroughly coated.
4. Spread the bread crumbs over the top of the pasta mixture.
5. Bake until bread crumbs are golden brown and sauce is bubbly, about 45 minutes.

Tuna Cashew Casserole

Ingredients:

1 (3 oz.) can chow mein noodles
1 (6 oz.) can chunk light tuna in water, drained
1 cup roasted salted cashews
1 cup diced celery
1 (10.75 oz.) can condensed cream of mushroom soup
1/4 cup water

Directions:

1. Preheat an oven to 375 degrees F (190 degrees C).
2. Measure 1/2 cup of the chow mein noodles and set aside.
3. Combine the remaining noodles, tuna, cashews, celery mushroom soup, and water in a 1 1/2 quart baking dish.
4. Top with the 1/2 cup of noodles you set aside.
5. Bake until heated through, about 30 minutes.

Spinach Tuna Casserole

Ingredients:

6 eggs
2 (10 oz.) pkgs. frozen chopped spinach, thawed and drained
2 tbsps. onion powder
1 (12 oz.) can tuna, drained
2 (10.75 oz.) cans condensed cream of mushroom soup
1 cup sour cream
1/4 cup butter, melted
4 slices soft bread, torn into small pieces

Directions:

1. Preheat oven to 350 degrees F (175 degrees C).
2. Place eggs in a saucepan and cover with cold water.
3. Bring water to a boil.
4. Cover pan, remove from heat, and let eggs stand in the hot water for 10 to 12 minutes.
5. Remove from water; peel and chop.
6. Combine the chopped eggs, spinach, onion powder, tuna, cream of mushroom soup, and sour cream in a 9x13 inch baking dish. Mix well.
7. Scatter bread pieces over tuna mix; drizzle with melted butter.
8. Bake until bread is toasted and casserole is hot, about 30 to 35 minutes.

Tuna Rice Puff Casserole

Ingredients:

2/3 cup uncooked white rice 1 1/3 cups water
1/3 cup butter
1/4 cup all-purpose flour
1 tsp. salt
1/4 tsp. ground black pepper
1 1/2 cups milk
2 egg yolks
1 (12 oz.) can tuna, undrained
2 tbsps. grated onion
1 tbsp. lemon juice
2 egg whites

Directions:

1. Bring the rice and water to a boil in a saucepan over high heat.
2. Reduce heat to medium-low, cover, and simmer until the rice is tender, and the liquid has been absorbed, 20 to 25 minutes. (See Cook's Note.)
3. Preheat oven to 350 degrees F (175 degrees C).
4. Melt the butter in a large saucepan over medium-low heat.
5. Whisk in the flour, salt, and pepper; cook and stir for 2 minutes.
6. Gradually whisk the milk into the flour mixture, and bring to a simmer over medium heat.
7. Cook, stirring frequently, until mixture has thickened slightly, about 3 minutes.
8. Remove from heat.
9. Whisk the egg yolks slightly in a medium bowl.
10. Gradually pour a steady stream of the hot milk mixture into the egg yolks, whisking constantly, until you have whisked in about half of the milk mixture.
11. Return the egg yolk mixture to the saucepan with the remaining milk, and whisk until smooth.
12. Cook 2 more minutes, stirring constantly.
13. Remove from heat.
14. Stir the rice, tuna, onion, and lemon juice into the milk mixture.
15. Beat egg whites until foamy in a large glass or metal mixing bowl.
16. Lift your beater or whisk straight up: the egg whites should form a sharp peak that holds its shape; set aside.
17. Gently fold in the egg whites until evenly blended, then pour into a 1 1/2 quart casserole dish.
18. Bake until the casserole has puffed slightly, is golden brown, and has set in the center, about 40 minutes.

Tomato Tuna Casserole

Ingredients:

1 (8 oz.) pkg. elbow macaroni
2 (8 oz.) cans tomato sauce
2 (7 oz.) cans tuna, drained
1 (8 oz.) container cottage cheese
1 onion, minced
1 (4 oz.) pkg. cream cheese, softened
1/4 cup sour cream
1 tsp. salt (optional)
1/2 cup bread crumbs
2 tbsps. butter, melted

Directions:

1. Bring a large pot of lightly salted water to a boil.
2. Cook elbow macaroni in the boiling water, stirring occasionally until cooked through but firm to the bite, 8 minutes.
3. Drain.
4. Preheat oven to 350 degrees F (175 degrees C).
5. Butter a 2 1/2-quart casserole dish.
6. Mix macaroni, tomato sauce, tuna, cottage cheese, onion, cream cheese, sour cream, and salt together in the prepared casserole dish. Stir bread crumbs and butter together in a bowl; spread over tuna mixture.
7. Bake until casserole is cooked through and bubbling, 35 to 40 minutes.

Cheese Lover's Tuna Casserole

Ingredients:

1 cup elbow macaroni
1 (10.75 oz.) can condensed cream of mushroom soup
2 (6 oz.) cans tuna, drained
1 lb. Cheddar cheese, cubed
1 1/2 cups seasoned croutons

Directions:

1. Preheat oven to 350 degrees F (175 degrees C).
2. Bring a large pot of lightly salted water to a boil.
3. Add pasta and cook for 8 to 10 minutes or until al dente; drain.
4. Meanwhile, in a 9x13 inch baking dish, combine soup, tuna and 1/2 of the cheese; mix well.
5. Add pasta to baking dish and mix together.
6. Add remaining cheese to the top of the mixture, then add croutons.
7. Cover dish and bake in preheated oven for 15 minutes or until the cheese is melted; serve.

Tuna Garden Casserole

Ingredients:

8 oz. penne pasta
1 tbsp. olive oil
1 large onion, chopped
2 stalks celery, chopped
1 red bell pepper, chopped
2 cloves garlic, crushed
Salt, to taste
Ground black pepper, to taste
1/4 cup sherry
1/2 lb. kale, stems removed and leaves coarsely chopped
1 (14.1 oz.) can potato leek soup
1 cup vegetable broth
1 (6 oz.) can tuna packed in water, drained
1 cup shredded mozzarella cheese
1/3 cup herb seasoned bread crumbs

Directions:

1. Preheat oven to 375 degrees F (190 degrees C). Lightly grease a 2 quart casserole dish.
2. Bring a large pot of salted water to a boil, add penne pasta, and cook 10 minutes or until al dente; drain.
3. Heat the oil in a large wok or skillet over medium-high heat.
4. Mix in onion and cook 5 minutes.
5. Stir in the celery and bell pepper and continue cooking for another five minutes.
6. Mix in the garlic, salt and pepper and continue cooking 3 minutes. Pour in sherry; stir in the kale and cover.
7. Reduce heat to medium and cook for 5 minutes, stirring occasionally, until the kale has wilted.
8. Transfer wok mixture to a large bowl.
9. Mix in the cooked pasta, soup, vegetable broth, and tuna.
10. Pour mixture into the prepared casserole dish. Top with a layer of mozzarella followed by a layer of bread crumbs.
11. Bake uncovered for 25 minutes.

Curry Tuna and Rice Casserole

Ingredients:

1 (10.75 oz.) can cream of celery soup
1 cup non-fat milk
1 tsp. curry powder
1/2 tsp. mustard powder
2 cups cooked white rice
2 (5 oz.) cans tuna, drained
1 small onion, chopped
1/4 cup bread crumbs
1 tbsp. butter, melted
1 tbsp. dried parsley
3 hard-boiled eggs, sliced

Directions:

1. Preheat oven to 350 degrees F (175 degrees C).
2. Mix cream of celery soup, milk, curry powder, and mustard powder in a large bowl.
3. Stir rice, tuna, and onion into the soup mixture; transfer to a casserole dish.
4. Mix bread crumbs, melted butter, and parsley in a bowl; sprinkle over tuna mixture.
5. Bake casserole in preheated oven until bread crumb mixture is golden brown, about 25 minutes.
6. Top with sliced eggs and return to over to bake another 5 minutes.
7. Let casserole cool 5 minutes before serving.

Portuguese Tuna Rice Casserole

Ingredients:

3 cups water
1 1/2 cups uncooked white rice
1 tbsp. butter
1 tbsp. olive oil
1 tbsp. olive oil
1 small onion, chopped
2 cloves garlic, minced
2 (5 oz.) cans tuna, drained
3/4 cup heavy cream
3 tbsps. ketchup
1 tsp. hot pepper sauce
Salt and pepper to taste
1/2 cup sliced black olives
1/2 cup shredded Cheddar cheese

Directions:

1. Preheat oven to 350 degrees F (175 degrees C).
2. Mix cream of celery soup, milk, curry powder, and mustard powder in a large bowl.
3. Stir rice, tuna, and onion into the soup mixture; transfer to a casserole dish.
4. Mix bread crumbs, melted butter, and parsley in a bowl.
5. Sprinkle over tuna mixture.
6. Bake casserole in preheated oven until bread crumb mixture is golden brown, about 25 minutes.
7. Top with sliced eggs and return to over to bake another 5 minutes.
8. Let casserole cool 5 minutes before serving.

Tuna Noodle Asparagus Casserole

Ingredients:

1 (6 oz.) pkg. wide egg noodles
1 (12 oz.) can white tuna in water, drained
1 (2.25 oz.) can sliced black olives
1 (10.75 oz.) can low-fat cream of mushroom soup
2 cups shredded sharp Cheddar cheese
5 dashes hot pepper sauce (such as Tabasco®), or to taste
ground black pepper to taste
1 (15 oz.) can asparagus spears, drained and cut into thirds

Directions:

1. Preheat oven to 350 degrees F (175 degrees C).
2. Bring a large pot of lightly salted water to a boil.
3. Cook egg noodles in the boiling water, stirring occasionally, until cooked through but firm to the bite, about 5 minutes; drain.
4. Stir noodles, tuna, black olives, and cream of mushroom soup together in the bottom of a casserole dish. Add 2/3 cup Cheddar cheese, hot pepper sauce, and black pepper to the noodle mixture; mix. Gently fold asparagus into the noodle mixture.
5. Sprinkle remaining Cheddar cheese over the dish.
6. Bake in preheated oven until hot and bubbly, about 30 minutes.

Mushroom Tuna Noodle Casserole

Ingredients:

5 cups dry egg noodles
1 (10.75 oz.) can condensed cream of mushroom soup
1 cup milk
1 1/2 cups water
2 (12 oz.) cans tuna, drained and flaked
1 (10 oz.) pkg. frozen green peas
1 (10 oz.) pkg. frozen carrots
2 (15 oz.) cans sliced potatoes, drained
Salt to taste
Ground black pepper to taste
Paprika to taste
3/4 cup dry bread crumbs

Directions:

1. Preheat oven to 350 degrees F (175 degrees C).
2. Bring a large pot of lightly salted water to a boil.
3. Add pasta and cook for 8 to 10 minutes or until al dente; drain.
4. In a mixing bowl combine soup, milk, and water.
5. Pour a small amount of the mixture into a 9x13 inch baking dish; enough to just cover the bottom.
6. Layer the cooked noodles, flaked tuna, peas, carrots, and potatoes until all used up.
7. Pour the remaining soup mixture over the layers.
8. Sprinkle with salt, pepper, and paprika. Lightly coat the entire casserole with bread crumbs.
9. Cover and bake in preheated oven for 45 minutes.

Tater Tot Casserole

Ingredients:

2 lbs. tater tots, thawed
1 (10.5 oz.) can condensed cream of chicken soup
1 cup finely chopped onion
1 (16 oz.) container sour cream
1 (8 oz.) pkg. sharp Cheddar cheese, shredded
1 dash garlic powder
1/2 tsp. seasoning salt
1/2 cup butter, softened
3 cups cornflakes cereal
1/2 cup butter, melted
2 tbsps. grated Parmesan cheese
Paprika to taste

Directions:

1. Preheat oven to 350 degrees F (175 degrees C).
2. Grease a 9x13 inch casserole dish.
3. In a large mixing bowl combine tater tots, soup, onion, sour cream, cheese, garlic powder, seasoning salt and softened butter; mix well. Transfer to casserole dish.
4. In a medium bowl combine cereal and melted butter; spread over casserole.
5. Sprinkle the top with parmesan cheese (use more or less according to your taste) and paprika.
6. Bake in preheated oven for 45 minutes to 1 hour, or until browned.

Chili Rellenos Casserole

Ingredients:

2 (7 oz.) cans whole green chile peppers, drained
8 oz. Monterey Jack cheese, shredded
8 oz. Longhorn or Cheddar cheese, shredded
2 eggs, beaten
1 (5 oz.) can evaporated milk
2 tbsps. all-purpose flour
1/2 cup milk
1 (8 oz.) can tomato sauce

Directions:

1. Preheat oven to 350 degrees F (175 degrees C).
2. Spray a 9x13-inch baking dish with cooking spray.
3. Lay half of the chilies evenly in bottom of baking dish.
4. Sprinkle with half of the Jack and Cheddar cheeses, and cover with remaining chilies.
5. In a bowl, mix together the eggs, milk, and flour, and pour over the top of the chilies.
6. Bake for 25 minutes.
7. Remove from oven, pour tomato sauce evenly over the top, and continue baking another 15 minutes. Sprinkle with remaining Jack and Cheddar cheeses, and serve.

Chili Dog Casserole

Ingredients:

8 hot dog buns 8 hot dogs
1 (15 oz.) can chili
1/4 cup chopped onion
1 tbsp. prepared mustard
2 cups shredded Cheddar cheese

Directions:

1. Preheat oven to 350 degrees F (175 degrees C).
2. Lightly grease a 9x13 inch baking dish.
3. Tear up the hot dog buns and arrange the pieces in the bottom of the dish evenly. Slice the hot dogs into bite size pieces and layer the pieces over the buns.
4. Pour the chili over the hot dogs, sprinkle with the chopped onion, then spread some mustard over the chili and the onion.
5. Top off with the cheese.
6. Bake at 350 degrees F (175 degrees C) for 30 minutes.

Corn Dog Casserole

Ingredients:

2 tbsps. butter
2 cups thinly sliced celery
1 1/2 cups sliced green onion
1 1/2 lbs. vegetarian hot dogs
2 eggs, beaten
1 1/2 cups milk
2 tsps. rubbed sage
1/4 tsp. ground black pepper
2 (8.5 oz.) pkgs. dry corn bread mix
2 cups shredded Cheddar cheese, divided

Directions:

1. Preheat oven to 400 degrees F (200 degrees C). Grease a shallow 3 quart baking dish.
2. In a large skillet over medium heat, melt butter, then saute celery for 5 minutes.
3. Stir in green onions, and saute an additional 5 minutes.
4. Place in a large bowl and set aside.
5. Cut hot dogs lengthwise into quarters, then cut into thirds.
6. In the same skillet, saute hot dogs for 5 minutes, until lightly browned.
7. Mix hot dogs into celery and onions. Set aside 1 cup of this mixture.
8. In a medium bowl, combine eggs, milk, sage, pepper, and corn bread mix.
9. Stir well to combine, then stir into remaining hot dog mixture.
10. Mix in 1 1/2 cups cheese. Spread mixture into prepared baking dish.
11. Top with reserved hot dog mixture and remaining 1/2 cup cheese.
12. Bake uncovered in preheated oven for 30 minutes, until golden brown.

Baked Corn Casserole

Ingredients:

1/4 cup butter
2 (3 oz.) pkgs. cream cheese
1 (11.25 oz.) can whole kernel corn, drained
1 (15 oz.) can cream-style corn
1 (4 oz.) can chopped green chile peppers
1/2 cup chopped onion
1 (6 oz.) can French-fried onions

Directions:

1. Preheat oven to 350 degrees F (175 degrees C).
2. In a medium size bowl, cream together butter and cream cheese.
3. Mix in whole kernel corn, cream-style corn, chiles, chopped onions, and 1/2 can of the French-fried onions.
4. Pour mixture into a 1 quart casserole dish.
5. Bake in a 350 degrees F (175 degrees C) oven for 15 minutes.
6. Remove from oven and sprinkle the remaining French-fried onions over the top of the casserole.
7. Return to the oven and bake an additional 15 minutes.

Cheesy Corn Casserole

Ingredients:

1 (11 oz.) can whole kernel corn, drained
1 (11 oz.) can cream-style corn
1 (8 oz.) container sour cream
1 egg
1 (8.5 oz.) pkg. dry corn bread mix
1 small onion, diced
1 cup shredded Cheddar cheese, divided

Directions:

1. Preheat oven to 350 degrees F (175 degrees C).
2. Grease a 9x13 inch baking dish.
3. In a large bowl combine whole corn, cream-style corn, sour cream, egg, dry corn bread mix, onion and 3/4 cup of Cheddar cheese.
4. Mix well and pour into prepared dish.
5. Bake in preheated oven for 25 minutes.
6. Remove from oven and sprinkle with remaining cheese.
7. Bake for another 20 minutes.

Mexican Beef and Corn Casserole

Ingredients:

1 lb. lean ground beef
1/3 cup chopped fresh cilantro (optional)
1 (15.5 oz.) can reduced sodium black beans, drained
1 (11 oz.) can Mexicorn, drained
2 tbsps. butter or margerine
1/2 cup salsa
2/3 cup fat-free sour cream
1/4 cup shredded low-fat Cheddar cheese

Directions:

1. Preheat oven to 400 degrees .
2. Cook ground beef in 12-inch nonstick skillet over medium-high heat, stirring frequently, until beef is done, about 5 minutes.
3. Remove from heat, then stir in cilantro.
4. Combine black beans, corn and butter in 8-inch baking dish.
5. Top with beef mixture; spread with salsa and sour cream and sprinkle with cheese.
6. Bake 20 minutes or until heated though and cheese is melted.

Chili Beef Casserole

Ingredients:

3/4 lb. lean ground beef
2 tsps. olive oil
2 onions, chopped
1 green bell pepper, chopped
1/4 cup frozen green peas
1/2 tsp. chili powder
1/2 tsp. red pepper flakes
1 (14.5 oz.) can canned tomatoes, drained and chopped
1/4 cup tomato paste
1 (15.25 oz.) can kidney beans, drained
1 (11 oz.) can whole kernel corn, drained
4 (6 inch) corn tortillas, quartered
1/3 cup shredded reduced-fat Cheddar cheese

Directions:

1. Preheat oven to 350 degrees F (175 degrees C).
2. Lightly grease a medium casserole dish.
3. In a skillet over medium heat, cook the ground beef until evenly brown.
4. Drain, and set aside.
5. Heat the olive oil in a separate skillet over medium heat, and cook the onions until tender. Mix in the green pepper and peas, and season with chili powder and red pepper flakes.
6. Stir the cooked beef, tomatoes, and tomato paste into the mixture.
7. Reduce heat to low, and simmer 5 minutes.
8. Mix in the kidney beans and corn.
9. Spoon 1/2 the skillet mixture into the prepared casserole dish, and top with 1/2 the tortilla quarters. Layer with remaining skillet mixture.
10. Cover and bake 25 minutes in the preheated oven.
11. Remove cover, and top with remaining tortillas and cheese.
12. Continue baking 10 minutes, or until cheese is melted and golden brown.

Beef Nacho Casserole

Ingredients:

1 lb. ground beef
1 1/2 cups chunky salsa
1 (10 oz.) can whole kernel corn, drained
3/4 cup creamy salad dressing (e.g. Miracle Whip)
1 tsp. chili powder
2 cups crushed tortilla chips
2 cups Colby cheese

Directions:

1. Preheat the oven to 350 degrees F (175 degrees C).
2. Place ground beef in a large skillet over medium-high heat.
3. Cook, stirring to crumble, until evenly browned.
4. Drain grease.
5. Remove from the heat, and stir the salsa, corn, mayonnaise and chili powder into the beef.
6. In a 2 quart casserole dish, layer the ground beef mixture, tortilla chips and cheese twice, ending with cheese on top.
7. Bake for 20 minutes uncovered in the preheated oven, until cheese is melted and dish is thoroughly heated.

Barbeque Beef Casserole

Ingredients:

2 lbs. ground beef
1 large onion, diced
1 green bell pepper, seeded and diced
1 (10 oz.) can whole kernel corn, drained
1/2 cup barbeque sauce
1 (14.5 oz.) can diced tomatoes, drained
3 (8.5 oz.) pkgs. corn bread mix

Directions:

1. Crumble the ground beef into a large skillet over medium-high heat.
2. Cook until evenly browned. Add the onion, bell pepper, corn and tomatoes.
3. Cook and stir until vegetables are tender.
4. Drain excess grease, and stir in the barbeque sauce.
5. Spread the beef mixture in an even layer in a 9x13 inch baking dish.
6. Prepare the cornbread batter mixes according to pkg. directions.
7. Spread the batter over the top of the beef mixture.
8. Bake for 20 to 25 minutes in the preheated oven, until the top is golden brown, and a knife inserted into the center of the cornbread layer comes out clean.

Beef Potato House Pie Casserole

Ingredients:

6 large potatoes, peeled and chopped
1/2 cup milk
2 tbsps. butter
2 lbs. ground beef
1 onion, chopped
1 green bell pepper, chopped salt and pepper to taste
1 (8 oz.) pkg. processed American cheese, sliced

Directions:

1. Preheat oven to 375 degrees F (190 degrees C).
2. Bring a large pot of salted water to a boil.
3. Add potatoes and cook until tender but still firm, about 15 minutes. Drain, then mash with milk and butter until smooth.
4. In a large, deep skillet over medium high heat, combine ground beef, onion and green pepper.
5. Cook until beef is evenly brown.
6. Drain excess fat. Season with salt and pepper.
7. In a deep casserole dish, spoon a layer of beef mixture.
8. Spread a layer of mashed potato over the beef.
9. Continue alternating layers until the dish is full.
10. Top with cheese.
11. Bake in preheated oven for 20 minutes.

Potato Pizza Casserole

Ingredients:

1 lb. ground beef
1 small onion, chopped
Salt and pepper to taste
1/4 tsp. garlic powder
5 cups peeled and thinly sliced potatoes
1 (3 oz.) pkg. chopped pepperoni
1 (10.75 oz.) can condensed tomato soup
1 (10.75 oz.) can condensed Cheddar cheese soup
1/2 cup milk
1/2 tsp. dried oregano
1/4 tsp. Italian seasoning
1/2 tsp. brown sugar
8 oz. shredded mozzarella cheese

Directions:

1. Spread the sliced potatoes in a layer on the bottom of a 9x13 inch baking dish.
2. Spread the ground beef and onion over the potatoes.
3. Place slices of pepperoni over the ground beef.
4. In a saucepan over medium heat, combine the tomato soup, Cheddar cheese soup, and milk. Season with oregano, Italian seasoning, and brown sugar.
5. Mix well, and cook until heated through. Pour over the contents of the baking dish.
6. Cover the dish with aluminum foil, and bake for 30 minutes in the preheated oven.
7. Remove the aluminum foil, sprinkle mozzarella cheese over the top, and bake for an additional 15 minutes, until the cheese is melted and bubbly.

Hamburger Potato Casserole

Ingredients:

1 lb. lean ground beef
3 cups peeled and thinly sliced potatoes
1 (10.75 oz.) can condensed cream of mushroom soup
1/2 cup chopped onion
3/4 cup milk
Salt to taste freshly ground pepper, to taste
1 cup shredded Cheddar cheese

Directions:

1. Preheat oven to 350 degrees F (175 degrees C).
2. In a medium skillet over medium heat, brown the ground beef; drain fat.
3. In a medium mixing bowl, combine cream of mushroom soup, onion, milk, salt and pepper to taste.
4. Alternately layer the potatoes, soup mixture and meat in a 11x7 inch (2 quart) baking dish.
5. Bake for 1 to 1 1/2 hours, or until potatoes are tender.
6. Top with Cheddar cheese, and continue baking until cheese is melted.

Pork Chop and Potato Casserole

Ingredients:

1 tbsp. vegetable oil
6 boneless pork chops
1 (10.75 oz.) can condensed cream of mushroom soup
1 cup milk
4 potatoes, thinly sliced
1/2 cup chopped onion
1 cup shredded Cheddar cheese

Directions:

1. Preheat oven to 400 degrees F (200 degrees C).
2. Heat oil in a large skillet over medium high-heat.
3. Place the pork chops in the oil, and sear.
4. In a medium bowl, combine the soup and the milk.
5. Arrange the potatoes and onions in a 9x13 inch baking dish.
6. Place the browned chops over the potatoes and onions, then pour the soup mixture over all.
7. Bake 30 minutes in the preheated oven.
8. Top with the cheese, and bake for 30 more minutes.

Hamburger Potato Casserole

Ingredients:

1 lb. lean ground beef
3 cups peeled and thinly sliced potatoes
1 (10.75 oz.) can condensed cream of mushroom soup
1/2 cup chopped onion
3/4 cup milk salt to taste
Freshly ground pepper, to taste
1 cup shredded Cheddar cheese

Directions:

1. Preheat oven to 350 degrees F (175 degrees C).
2. In a medium skillet over medium heat, brown the ground beef; drain fat.
3. In a medium mixing bowl, combine cream of mushroom soup, onion, milk, salt and pepper to taste.
4. Alternately layer the potatoes, soup mixture and meat in a 11x7 inch (2 quart) baking dish.
5. Bake for 1 to 1 1/2 hours, or until potatoes are tender.
6. Top with Cheddar cheese, and continue baking until cheese is melted.

Ham and Potato Casserole

Ingredients:

6 small potatoes, peeled and cubed
3 tbsps. butter
2 cups cubed cooked ham
1 small onion, finely chopped
1/4 cup butter
3 tbsps. all-purpose flour
Salt and ground black pepper to taste
1 (8 oz.) pkg. shredded Cheddar cheese
1/4 cup bread crumbs

Directions:

1. Place potatoes into a large pot and cover with salted water.
2. Bring to a boil.
3. Reduce heat to medium-low and simmer until tender, about 20 minutes.
4. Drain.
5. Preheat oven to 350 degrees F (175 degrees C).
6. Grease a 1 1/2-quart baking dish.
7. Melt 3 tbsps. butter in a skillet over medium heat. Stir in the ham and onion.
8. Cook and stir until the onion has softened and turned translucent, about 5 minutes.
9. Stir potatoes into ham mixture; transfer to the prepared baking dish.
10. Melt 1/4 cup butter in a saucepan over medium heat.
11. Stir flour into melted butter until smooth.
12. Gradually whisk milk into flour mixture; season with salt and black pepper.
13. Continue cooking and stirring until thickened, about 2 minutes.
14. Reduce heat to medium-low and stir Cheddar cheese into the white sauce until melted.
15. Pour sauce over ham and potatoes.
16. Sprinkle bread crumbs atop casserole.
17. Bake until sauce is bubbly and browned, 25 to 30 minutes.

Ham, Potato and Broccoli Casserole

Ingredients:

1 (16 oz.) pkg. frozen French fries
1 (16 oz.) pkg. frozen chopped broccoli
1 1/2 cups cooked, cubed ham
1 (10.75 oz.) can condensed cream of mushroom soup
1 (10.75 oz.) can milk
1/4 cup mayonnaise
1 cup grated Parmesan cheese

Directions:

1. Preheat oven to 375 degrees F (190 degrees C).
2. Spray a 9x13 inch baking dish with cooking spray.
3. Cover bottom of dish with layer of French fries.
4. Add a layer of broccoli, then sprinkle ham evenly over broccoli.
5. In a small bowl mix together soup, milk and mayonnaise.
6. Pour mixture evenly over ingredients in baking dish and sprinkle with cheese.
7. Bake uncovered in preheated oven for 40 minutes.

Ham and Swiss Casserole

Ingredients:

2 cups egg noodles
2 tbsps. vegetable oil
1 cup chopped onions
1 (6 oz.) can mushrooms, drained
1 cup diced cooked ham
1 cup diced Swiss cheese
1 tsp. salt
1/2 tsp. ground black pepper
2 eggs
1/4 cup milk
1/4 cup grated Parmesan cheese

Directions:

1. Bring a large pot of lightly salted water to a boil.
2. Add egg noodles and cook for 8 to 10 minutes or until al dente; drain.
3. Preheat oven to 400 degrees F (200 degrees C).
4. Toss drained noodles with 2 tsps. of the oil.
5. Heat remaining oil in a skillet and saute onion over medium heat until soft. Combine noodles, onion, mushrooms, ham, Swiss cheese, salt and pepper. Transfer to a greased 3 quart casserole dish. In a bowl mix together egg and milk; pour over noodle mixture.
6. Sprinkle with parmesan cheese.
7. Bake for 30 minutes.

Ham and Noodle Casserole

Ingredients:

6 cups water
4 cups uncooked egg noodles
1 onion, chopped
1/2 cup sour cream
1 (10.75 oz.) can condensed cream of chicken soup
2 cups diced cooked ham
2 cups shredded Swiss cheese
Salt and pepper to taste
1/4 cup dry bread crumbs

Directions:

1. Preheat an oven to 350 degrees F (175 degrees C).
2. Grease a 2-quart casserole.
3. Bring water to a full rolling boil in a pot..
4. Cook the egg noodles in the boiling water, stirring occasionally, for 3 minutes; remove from heat, cover, and let stand until the noodles are tender, about 10 minutes.
5. Drain.
6. Stir the noodles, onion, sour cream, chicken soup, ham, and Swiss cheese together in a large bowl. Season with salt and pepper.
7. Spoon into the prepared casserole. Sprinkle the top with bread crumbs.
8. Bake until the casserole is bubbling and the bread crumbs have browned, about 40 minutes.

Pierogi Casserole

Ingredients:

5 potatoes, peeled and cubed
1/2 cup milk
1/2 cup butter, melted
1/2 lb. bacon, diced
1 onion, chopped
6 cloves garlic, minced
1/2 (16 oz.) pkg. lasagna noodles
2 cups shredded Cheddar cheese
Salt and pepper to taste
1 (8 oz.) container sour cream
3 tbsps. chopped fresh chives

Directions:

1. Preheat oven to 350 degrees F (175 degrees C).
2. Place the potatoes in a large pot with water to cover over high heat.
3. Bring to a boil and cook until the potatoes are tender.
4. Remove from heat, drain, then combine with the milk and 6 tbsps. of butter, mash and set aside.
5. Melt the remaining 2 tbsps. of the butter in a large skillet over medium high heat.
6. Saute the bacon, onion and garlic in the butter for 5 to 10 minutes, or until the bacon is fully cooked.
7. Cook the lasagna noodles according to pkg. directions and cool under running water.
8. Place 1/2 of the mashed potatoes into the bottom of a 9x13 inch baking dish.
9. Top this with 1/3 of the cheese, followed by a layer of lasagna noodles.
10. Repeat this with the remaining potatoes, another 1/3 of the cheese and a layer of noodles.
11. Then arrange the bacon, onion and garlic over the noodles, then another layer of noodles, and finally top all with the remaining cheese. Season with salt and pepper to taste.
12. Bake, uncovered, at 350 degrees F (175 degrees C) for 30 to 45 minutes, or until the cheese is melted and bubbly. Serve with sour cream and chopped fresh chives.

Pineapple Casserole

Ingredients:

1 (20 oz.) can pineapple chunks, drained
1 (8 oz.) can crushed pineapple with juice
2 tbsps. all-purpose flour
1 cup white sugar
1 1/2 cups shredded Cheddar cheese
1 2/3 cups crushed saltine crackers
3 tbsps. butter, melted

Directions:

1. Preheat oven to 350 degrees F (175 degrees C).
2. Combine the pineapple chunks and crushed pineapple with syrup.
3. Mix together and pour into a 2 quart baking dish.
4. Mix together the flour and sugar, sprinkle evenly on top of pineapple.
5. Cover with cheese, top cheese with cracker crumbs and drizzle melted butter on top.
6. Bake at 350 degrees F (175 degrees C) for 25 minutes. Allow to cool for 10 minutes and serve.

Bean Casserole

Ingredients:

2 tbsps. olive oil
1 large onion, sliced
1 medium carrot, sliced
2 cloves garlic, finely chopped
1 tsp. white sugar
1 red bell pepper, seeded and chopped
6 fresh mushrooms, sliced
1 tbsp. all-purpose flour
1/2 cup water
1 tbsp. tomato paste
1/2 tsp. dried basil
1/4 tsp. dried thyme
1 (14.5 oz.) can red kidney beans, drained
1/2 tsp. salt ground black pepper to taste
1/2 (1 lb.) loaf French bread, cut into
1/2 inch thick slices
1 tbsp. olive oil
1/4 cup grated Parmesan cheese

Directions:

1. Preheat the oven to 450 degrees F (230 degrees C).
2. Heat 2 tbsps. of olive oil in a large skillet over medium heat.
3. Add the onion, garlic and carrot; cook and stir until onion is tender and transparent. Stir in the sugar, red pepper and mushrooms and continue to cook until onion is browned.
4. Sprinkle the flour over the vegetables and stir to blend. Cook for 1 minute then mix in the water and tomato paste. Season with basil and thyme. Mix in the beans and season with salt and pepper. Transfer to a greased casserole dish.
5. Pour the remaining oil into a shallow dish. Dip one side of each slice of bread in the oil, then arrange on top of the casserole with the oiled side up. Sprinkle Parmesan cheese over the top.
6. Bake for 10 to 15 minutes in the preheated oven, until the bread and cheese are toasted.

Spinach and Bean Casserole

Ingredients:

1 cup dry black-eyed peas
1/4 cup olive oil
1 onion, chopped
3 cups fresh spinach
1 (28 oz.) can peeled and diced tomatoes
2 tsps. salt
1 tsp. fennel seed, ground

Directions:

1. Preheat oven to 350 degrees F (175 degrees C).
2. Cook black-eye peas in a pressure cooker for 12 minutes.
3. Heat oil in a large saucepan over medium high heat.
4. Saute onion with spinach, tomatoes, salt and fennel for 15 minutes.
5. Combine beans with spinach mixture in a 2 quart casserole dish.
6. Bake in preheated oven for 15 minutes.

Oyster Casserole

Ingredients:

1 cup butter, melted
1/2 (16 oz.) pkg. saltine crackers, crushed
2 (8 oz.) cans oysters
1 1/2 tbsps. heavy whipping cream
1 tsp. Worcestershire sauce
2 (14.75 oz.) cans cream-style corn

Directions:

1. Preheat oven to 425 degrees F (220 degrees C).
2. Grease a 9x13 inch casserole dish. Drain the oysters, reserving juice.
3. In a small mixing bowl combine margarine and crushed saltine crackers.
4. Cut the oysters into small pieces, set aside. In a small mixing bowl combine cream, oyster juice and Worcestershire sauce.
5. Spread one can of corn onto the bottom of the casserole dish. Layer 1/2 of the oysters over the corn, 1/2 of the cracker mixture.
6. Repeat layering with remaining ingredients.
7. Pour the oyster juice mixture over the top of the entire casserole. Cover the casserole dish with aluminum foil.
8. Bake casserole for 20 minutes.
9. Remove foil and bake an additional 30 minutes.

Mediterranean Casserole

Ingredients:

1 lb. potatoes
3 tbsps. extra-virgin olive oil
4 (4.375 oz.) cans sardines, drained
1/2 lb. cherry tomatoes, diced
2 cloves garlic, chopped
1 tbsp. dried basil
2 tbsps. bread crumbs

Directions:

1. Place the potatoes into a large pot and cover with salted water.
2. Bring to a boil.
3. Reduce heat to medium-low, cover, and simmer until tender, about 20 minutes.
4. Drain. Cover with cold water and allow to sit until cool, draining and replacing the cold water as needed.
5. Peel and slice the potatoes thinly.
6. Preheat an oven to 350 degrees F (175 degrees C).
7. Grease a casserole dish with the olive oil. Line the casserole dish with an even layer of potato slices; top with a layer of sardine fillets.
8. Scatter the diced tomatoes over the sardines.
9. Sprinkle the garlic, basil, and bread crumbs over the tomatoes.
10. Bake until heated through, about 20 minutes.

Italian Casserole

Ingredients:

3/4 lb. lean ground beef
1 onion, chopped
1 (28 oz.) can whole peeled tomatoes, chopped
1 (6 oz.) can tomato paste
1 tsp. salt
1 tbsp. dried parsley
1/2 tsp. garlic
Salt black pepper to taste
8 oz. wide egg noodles
1 (12 oz.) pkg. sharp cheddar cheese singles

Directions:

1. In large skillet, brown ground beef and onion.
2. Stir in tomatoes, tomato paste, salt, parsley, garlic salt and pepper, and simmer over low heat for 3 hours.
3. Preheat oven to 350 degrees F (175 degrees C).
4. Bring a large pot of lightly salted water to a boil.
5. Add pasta and cook for 8 to 10 minutes or until al dente.
6. Drain.
7. In a 2 quart casserole dish, combine noodles and meat mixture.
8. Top with cheese slices and bake for 15 to 20 minutes, or until cheese is melted.

Meatball Sandwich Casserole

Ingredients:

1/3 cup chopped green onions
1/4 cup Italian seasoned bread crumbs
3 tbsps. grated Parmesan cheese
1 lb. ground beef
1 (1 lb.) loaf Italian bread, cut into 1-inch cubes
1 (8 oz.) pkg. cream cheese, softened
1/2 cup mayonnaise
1 tsp. Italian seasoning
1/4 tsp. freshly ground black pepper
2 cups shredded mozzarella cheese
3 cups spaghetti sauce
1 cup water
2 cloves garlic, minced

Directions:

1. Preheat oven to 400 degrees F (205 degrees C).
2. Mix together onions, bread crumbs, Parmesan cheese and ground beef.
3. Roll into 1 inch diameter balls, and place in a baking pan.
4. Bake for 15 to 20 minutes, or until beef is no longer pink.
5. Reduce the oven temperature to 350 degrees F (175 degrees C).
6. Arrange the bread cubes in a single layer in an ungreased 9x13 inch baking dish.
7. Mix together the cream cheese, mayonnaise, Italian seasoning and black pepper until smooth.
8. Spread this mixture over each bread cube. Sprinkle with 1/2 cup of the grated mozzarella cheese.
9. In a large bowl, mix together spaghetti sauce, water, and garlic.
10. Gently stir in meatballs. Pour over the bread and cheese mixture in the baking pan.
11. Sprinkle the remaining mozzarella cheese evenly over the top.
12. Bake at 350 degrees F (175 degrees C) for 30 minutes, or until heated through.

Lentil Casserole

Ingredients:

1 (16 oz.) pkg. dry lentils
2 cups water
1 (29 oz.) can crushed tomatoes
1 cup chopped carrots
1 cup chopped green bell pepper
1 cup chopped fresh mushrooms
1 cup chopped onion
1/2 cup chopped celery
2 tsps. dried parsley
2 cloves garlic, minced
1 cup shredded reduced-fat Cheddar

Directions:

1. Preheat oven to 375 degrees F (190 degrees C).
2. Spread lentils into a shallow 2-quart baking dish.
3. Pour water over lentils. Add tomatoes, carrots, green bell pepper, mushrooms, onion, celery, parsley, and garlic to lentil mixture.
4. Cover dish with aluminum foil.
5. Bake until lentils are tender, 1 1/2 to 2 hours.
6. Remove aluminum foil and sprinkle Cheddar cheese over casserole.
7. Bake until cheese is melted, about 5 minutes more.

Cauliflower Casserole

Ingredients:

1 head cauliflower, separated into florets
1 cup sour cream
1 cup shredded Cheddar cheese
1/2 cup crushed corn flakes
1/4 cup finely chopped green bell pepper
1/4 cup finely chopped red bell pepper
1 tsp. salt
1/4 cup grated Parmesan cheese
Paprika (optional)

Directions:

1. Preheat oven to 325 degrees F (165 degrees C).
2. Grease a 2 quart baking dish.
3. Place a steamer insert into a saucepan, and fill with water to just below the bottom of the steamer.
4. Cover, and bring the water to a boil over high heat.
5. Add the cauliflower, and steam until crisp-tender, about 5 minutes. Drain, and set aside.
6. Combine sour cream, Cheddar cheese, corn flakes, bell peppers, and salt in a medium bowl.
7. Stir in the cauliflower, and transfer to the prepared baking dish.
8. Sprinkle Parmesan cheese and paprika over the top of the dish.
9. Bake uncovered until heated through, 30 to 35 minutes.

Sauerkraut Casserole

Ingredients:

1 lb. sauerkraut
14 oz. tomato, coarsely chopped
1 cup white sugar
6 slices bacon, diced
1 tbsp. ground black pepper

Directions:

1. Preheat oven to 325 degrees F (165 degrees C).
2. Combine sauerkraut, tomatoes, sugar, bacon, and black pepper in a 9x13 inch casserole dish.
3. Bake for 2 hours and 15 minutes.
4. When finished cooking it should be bubbly around the edges and caramelized on top.

Crab Casserole

Ingredients:

1 (14.5 oz.) can green beans
2 (6 oz.) cans crabmeat
3 tsps. all-purpose flour, divided
1 (8 oz.) pkg. Cheddar cheese, shredded
1 (6 oz.) can French-fried onion rings
1 (10.25 oz.) can condensed tomato soup
1 (10.75 oz.) can milk
1 (10 oz.) can refrigerated biscuit

Directions:

1. Preheat oven to 350 degrees F (175 degrees C).
2. In a 2 quart casserole layer the beans, crab, 1 tsp. flour, cheese and all but 1/3 cup onion rings.
3. In a small bowl mix together the soup and milk; stir in remaining 2 tsps. flour and pour mixture over casserole.
4. Bake for 10 minutes or until bubbly.
5. Arrange biscuits on top of casserole and bake for another 20 minutes, adding remaining onion rings in the last 3 minutes of baking.

Shrimp and Crab Casserole

Ingredients:

2 cups water
1 cup uncooked white rice
1 lb. crab meat
2 (12 oz.) pkgs. frozen shrimp, thawed
2 cups mayonnaise
1 cup chopped onion
2 cups milk
1 tsp. hot pepper sauce
1/2 cup sliced almonds
10 buttery round crackers, crushed

Directions:

1. Preheat oven to 350 degrees F (175 degrees C).
2. Lightly grease a 3 quart casserole dish.
3. In a saucepan, bring water to a boil.
4. Add rice and stir.
5. Reduce heat, cover and simmer for 20 minutes.
6. Combine crab meat, shrimp, rice, mayonnaise, onion, milk, hot sauce, and almonds in casserole dish. Mix well.
7. Cover top of casserole with crumbled crackers.
8. Bake, uncovered, in preheated oven for 30 to 40 minutes, or until casserole is bubbling.

Baked Spaghetti Casserole

Ingredients:

4 eggs, beaten
2/3 cup Parmesan cheese
2 tbsps. butter
1 cup cottage cheese,
1 (28 oz.) jar spaghetti sauce
1 cup shredded mozzarella cheese

Directions:

1. Preheat oven to 350 degrees F (175 degrees C).
2. Prepare a 9x13-inch baking dish with cooking spray.
3. Bring a large pot of lightly salted water to a boil.
4. Cook spaghetti in the boiling water, stirring occasionally until cooked through but firm to the bite, about 12 minutes.
5. Drain and transfer to a large bowl.
6. Mix eggs, Parmesan cheese, and butter with the spaghetti to coat pasta completely; spread into the prepared baking dish.
7. Spread cottage cheese over the spaghetti to cover completely.
8. Spread spaghetti sauce over the cottage cheese; top with a layer of mozzarella cheese.
9. Bake until hot in the center, about 30 minutes.

Cowboy Casserole

Ingredients:

1/2 lb. bacon
1 lb. ground beef
1 small onion, chopped
2 (15 oz.) cans baked beans with pork
1/3 cup barbeque sauce
1 (7.5 oz.) pkg. refrigerated biscuit dough

Directions:

1. Cook bacon in a large skillet or Dutch oven over medium heat until evenly browned.
2. Drain, and cut into bite size pieces.
3. Set aside.
4. Add hamburger and onion to the skillet, and cook until no longer pink, and the onion is tender.
5. Drain.
6. Stir bacon, baked beans and barbeque sauce into the ground beef, and bring to a boil.
7. Reduce heat to medium low, and place biscuits in a single layer over the top of the mixture.
8. Cover, and simmer for about 10 minutes, or until the biscuits are done. Place two biscuits on each plate, and spoon beans over.

Chow Mein Noodle Casserole

Ingredients:

1 lb. ground beef
1 onion, chopped
2 stalks celery, chopped
1/2 cup slivered almonds
1 cup cooked rice
1 (10.75 oz.) can condensed cream of chicken soup
1/2 cup water
3 tbsps. soy sauce
5 oz. chow mein noodles

Directions:

1. Preheat oven to 350 degrees F (175 degrees C).
2. In a large skillet over medium high heat, saute the ground beef for 5 minutes.
3. Add the onion and celery and saute for 5 more minutes.
4. In a separate medium bowl, combine the almonds, rice, soup, water and soy sauce.
5. Mix together well and add to the beef mixture.
6. Place this into a lightly greased 9x13 inch baking dish. Top with chow mein noodles.
7. Bake at 350 degrees F (175 degrees C) for 20 minutes.

Reuben Casserole

Ingredients:

6 slices rye bread, cubed
1 (16 oz.) can sauerkraut, drained and rinsed
1 lb. deli sliced corned beef, cut into strips
3/4 cup Russian-style salad dressing
2 cups shredded Swiss cheese

Directions:

1. Preheat oven to 400 degrees F.
2. Spread bread cubes in a large casserole dish.
3. Spread sauerkraut evenly over the bread cubes, then layer beef strips
4. over sauerkraut.
5. Pour dressing over all.
6. Cover with aluminum foil.
7. Bake for 20 minutes.
8. Remove cover.
9. Sprinkle with cheese.
10. Bake uncovered for another 10 minutes, or until cheese is melted and bubbly.
11. Serve and enjoy!

Sloppy Joe Casserole

Ingredients:

1 lb. ground beef
½ cup medium onion, chopped
1 can (15 oz.) tomato sauce
1 tbsps. packed brown sugar
2 tsp. Worcestershire sauce
1 tsp. yellow mustard
1 pkg. corn bread muffin mix
1/3 cup milk
2 tbsps. vegetable oil
1 egg
1 cup shredded Cheddar cheese

Directions:

1. Heat oven to 350 degrees F.
2. In large non-stick skillet, cook beef and onion over medium-high heat 5 to 7 minutes, stirring frequently, until brown.
3. Drain.
4. Stir in tomato sauce, brown sugar, Worcestershire sauce and mustard.
5. Cook 2 to 3 minutes, stirring frequently, until boiling.
6. In small bowl, stir corn bread mix, milk, oil and egg just until moistened (batter will be lumpy).
7. Spoon hot beef mixture a large casserole dish.
8. Sprinkle with 3/4 cup of the cheese.
9. Spoon corn bread batter evenly over top.
10. Bake 25 to 35 minutes or until toothpick inserted in center of topping comes out clean.
11. Sprinkle remaining 1/4 cup cheese while hot.
12. Serve and enjoy!

Frito Casserole

Ingredients:

1 lb. ground beef
1 can tomato soup
2 cans chili with beans
1 med. onion, chopped
1 bag Frito-Lay Frito Chips
1 pkg. sharp Cheddar cheese, shredded

Directions:

1. Preheat oven to 350 degrees F.
2. Meanwhile, brown beef and onions in a large skillet.
3. Drain.
4. Add soup and chili to beef.
5. Simmer for 10 minutes.
6. Spray a large casserole dish with cooking spray.
7. Line the bottom of the pan with Fritos.
8. Pour mixture into pan.
9. Cover top of mixture with Fritos and cheese.
10. Bake for 20 minutes, or until cheese is golden brown.

Chickpea Casserole

Ingredients:

3 (15 oz.) cans chickpeas, drained
1 cup cooked brown rice
4 large shallots, minced or grated
2 cloves garlic, minced
Juice and zest of 1 lemon
Salt and pepper
2 large eggs, beaten
1 cup small curd cottage cheese
3/4 cup full fat plain yogurt (not Greek yogurt)
1 cup grated Parmesan cheese, divided
1/2 cup fresh parsley
2 stalks fresh rosemary leaves
2/3 cup dried bread crumbs
Olive oil

Directions:

1. Preheat the oven to 375 degrees F.
2. Lightly grease a 9 x 13" casserole dish with olive oil.
3. In a large bowl, mix together the chickpeas, rice, shallots, garlic, and lemon zest and juice.
4. Season with salt and pepper to taste.
5. In a medium bowl, mix the eggs, cottage cheese, yogurt, and 1/2 cup of the Parmesan cheese.
6. Finely mince the parsley and rosemary leaves.
7. Stir the cottage cheese mixture and herbs into the chickpea mixture.
8. Spread the mixture in the prepared baking dish and top with the remaining 1/2 cup Parmesan and the bread crumbs.
9. Drizzle with olive oil.
10. Bake for 45 minutes, or until bubbling and golden.
11. Let stand for 10 minutes.
12. Serve and enjoy!

Philly Cheesesteak Casserole

Ingredients:

1 lb. of macaroni, cooked and drained
4 tbsp. butter, divided
1 8 oz. container fajita medley (sliced green peppers, red peppers, and onion)
2 lbs. shaved steak
2 cups whole milk
2 tbsps. flour
2 tsp. dry mustard
Salt & pepper to taste
2 oz. cream cheese
2 (7 oz.) pkgs. sliced pepper jack cheese
8 oz. sharp Cheddar cheese, shredded

Directions:

1. Prepare macaroni according to the package directions.
2. Drain and set aside.
3. Melt 2 tbsps. of butter in a large skillet and sauté the vegetables for 7 minutes then add steak.
4. Cook over medium-high heat until meat is brown and vegetables are tender, stirring often.
5. Set the meat/veggies mix aside.
6. Preheat the oven to 350 degrees F.
7. Add 2 tbsps. of butter and milk to a large saucepan.
8. Cook over medium heat, stirring constantly, until butter is melted.
9. Whisk in the flour, dry mustard, salt and pepper, 1 package sliced pepper jack cheese (torn in to chunks) and cream cheese.
10. Stir until smooth and thickened.
11. Pour the sauce mixture over the macaroni and stir to mix it.
12. Add the vegetable/meat mixture and stir to incorporate.
13. Transfer half of the macaroni/vegetable/meat mixture to a 9 x 13" baking dish.
14. Top with sliced pepper-jack cheese (about 5 slices) and sprinkle with a handful of sharp cheddar cheese.
15. Add remaining macaroni mixture and top with the remaining cheeses.
16. Cover with tin foil and bake for 15 minutes.
17. Remove tin foil and broil for 5 minutes or until the top is brown and bubbly.

Eggs and Bacon Casserole

Ingredients:

4 bacon strips
18 large eggs
1 cup milk
1 cup (4 oz.) shredded cheddar cheese
1 cup (8 oz.) sour cream
1/4 cup sliced green onions
1 to 1-1/2 tsps. salt
1/2 tsp. pepper

Directions:

1. Preheat oven to 325 degrees F.
2. In a large skillet, cook bacon over medium heat until crisp.
3. Remove to paper towel to drain.
4. In a large bowl, beat eggs.
5. Add milk, cheese, sour cream, onions, salt and pepper.
6. Pour into a greased 13 x 9".baking dish.
7. Crumble bacon and sprinkle on top.
8. Bake, uncovered, for 40-45 minutes or until knife inserted near the
9. center comes out clean.
10. Let stand for 5 minutes.
11. Serve and enjoy!

Vegetarian Chili Casserole

Ingredients:

Olive spray oil
1 pkg. cornbread mix.
1 (15-oz.) can vegetarian bean chili
1 (15-oz.) can kidney or black beans, drained
1 (12.5-oz.) jar medium salsa
1 1/2 cup shredded Monterey Jack & Cheddar cheese
3 green onions, sliced

Directions:

1. Make cornbread according to package directions.
2. Preheat the oven to 350 degrees F.
3. Lightly spray a large baking dish with cooking spray.
4. Crumble half of the cornbread into the baking dish.
5. Combine chili, beans and salsa in a large bowl.
6. Spoon chili mixture evenly over cornbread.
7. Crumble remaining cornbread over chili mixture. Sprinkle with cheese.
8. Bake in the top third of the oven for 30 minutes, until cheese is melted and top is golden brown.
9. Allow to sit 5 to 10 minutes before serving.
10. Sprinkle sliced green onions on top.
11. Serve and enjoy!

Sweet Potato Casserole

Ingredients:

5 sweet potatoes, peeled and sliced
1/2 cup packed brown sugar
1/4 cup low fat margarine
2 tbsps. orange juice
2 pinches ground cinnamon
1 (10.5 oz.) package miniature marshmallows

Directions:

1. Preheat oven to 350 degrees F (175 degrees C).
2. Boil sliced sweet potatoes in water until tender.
3. Drain.
4. In a large bowl, blend the potatoes until creamy.
5. Stir in the butter, brown sugar, orange juice to taste and a dash of ground cinnamon.
6. Spread the sweet potato mixture into a 9x13 inch pan.
7. Sprinkle the miniature marshmallows over the top and bake until golden brown.

Sweet Potato and Apple Casserole

Ingredients:

3 sweet potatoes, peeled and quartered
1/2 cup firmly packed brown sugar
1 tsp. ground cinnamon
1 tsp. ground nutmeg
2 large cooking apples, peeled, cored and cut into 1/4 inch rings
1/4 cup all-purpose flour
1/4 cup firmly packed brown sugar
1/4 cup butter
1/4 cup chopped pecans Add all ingredients to list

Directions:

1. Place sweet potatoes in a large saucepan with enough water to cover.
2. Bring to a boil and cook 25 minutes, or until tender but firm.
3. Drain, cool and cut into 1/4 inch slices.
4. Preheat oven to 350 degrees F (175 degrees C).
5. Lightly grease a 7x11 inch baking dish.
6. In a small bowl, mix brown sugar, cinnamon and nutmeg.
7. Layer sweet potatoes, brown sugar mixture and apples in the prepared baking dish.
8. In a medium bowl, mix flour, brown sugar, butter and pecans.
9. Sprinkle over the sweet potatoes.
10. Bake 30 minutes, or until lightly browned.

Sweet Potato Pineapple Casserole

Ingredients:

3 sweet potatoes
1/2 cup crushed pineapple with juice
1/4 cup packed light brown sugar
3 tbsps. butter

Directions:

1. Preheat oven to 350 degrees F (175 degrees C).
2. Lightly grease a 9x13 inch baking dish.
3. In a large soup pot, boil sweet potatoes whole until soft.
4. Remove skins, and dice into bite-sized pieces.
5. Mix sweet potatoes, crushed pineapple, light brown sugar, and butter in prepared baking dish.
6. Bake for 45 minutes, or until casserole is mushy with no excess water in the dish.

Yellow Squash Casserole

Ingredients:

4 cups sliced yellow squash
1/2 cup chopped onion
35 buttery round crackers, crushed
1 cup shredded Cheddar cheese
2 eggs, beaten
3/4 cup milk
1/4 cup butter, melted
1 tsp. salt
Ground black pepper to taste
2 tbsps. butter

Directions:

1. Preheat oven to 400 degrees F (200 degrees C).
2. Place squash and onion in a large skillet over medium heat.
3. Pour in a small amount of water.
4. Cover, and cook until squash is tender, about 5 minutes.
5. Drain well, and place in a large bowl.
6. In a medium bowl, mix together cracker crumbs and cheese.
7. Stir half of the cracker mixture into the cooked squash and onions. In a small bowl, mix together eggs and milk, then add to squash mixture.
8. Stir in 1/4 cup melted butter, and season with salt and pepper.
9. Spread into a 9x13 inch baking dish.
10. Sprinkle with remaining cracker mixture, and dot with 2 tbsps. butter.
11. Bake in preheated oven for 25 minutes, or until lightly browned.

Zucchini Cornbread Casserole

Ingredients:

4 cups shredded zucchini
1 onion, chopped
2 eggs, beaten
1 (8.5 oz.) package dry corn muffin mix
1/2 tsp. salt
1/4 tsp. ground black pepper
8 oz. Cheddar cheese, shredded

Directions:

1. In a large bowl mix together the zucchini, onion, eggs, muffin mix, salt and pepper.
2. Stir in 4 oz. of the cheese. Spread this mixture into a greased 2 quart casserole dish.
3. Top with remaining 4 oz. of cheese.
4. Bake in a preheated oven for 60 minutes.

Broccoli Casserole

Ingredients:

3 tbsps. butter
1 onion, chopped
2 (10 oz.) packages chopped frozen broccoli, thawed
1 (10.75 oz.) can condensed cream of mushroom soup
1 cup shredded sharp Cheddar cheese
1 cup mayonnaise 2 eggs, beaten
1/2 tsp. garlic salt
1/4 tsp. ground black pepper
1/2 tsp. seasoned salt
1 1/2 tsps. lemon juice
12 buttery round crackers, crushed fine
2 tbsps. butter

Directions:

1. Preheat oven to 350 degrees F (175 degrees C).
2. Melt 3 tbsps. butter in a medium skillet over medium-high heat.
3. Saute onion until golden.
4. In a 2 quart casserole dish, mix together onion, broccoli, soup, cheese, mayonnaise, eggs, garlic salt, pepper, seasoned salt, and lemon juice.
5. Sprinkle crushed crackers over top and dot with remaining 2 tbsps. butter.

Green Bean Casserole

Ingredients:

2 (14.5 oz.) cans green beans, drained
1 (10.75 oz.) can condensed cream of mushroom soup
1 (6 oz.) can French fried onions
1 cup shredded Cheddar cheese

Directions:

1. Preheat oven to 350 degrees F (175 degrees C).
2. Place green beans and soup in a large microwave-safe bowl.
3. Mix well and heat in the microwave on high until warm (3 to 5 minutes).
4. Stir in 1/2 cup of cheese and heat mixture for another 2 to 3 minutes.
5. Transfer green bean mixture to a casserole dish and sprinkle with French fried onions and remaining cheese.
6. Bake until the cheese melts and the onions just begin to brown.

Pulled Pork Casserole

Ingredients:

6 slices bacon
2/3 cup milk
1 cup shredded pepper Jack cheese
4 oz. cream cheese, cut into cubes
1/2 tsp. pepper
3 cups shredded Cheddar cheese
1 pkg. (8 oz.) sour cream
1 can (4.5 oz.) chopped green chilies, drained
3 cups shredded barbecue pork
3/4 cup barbecue sauce
Chopped fresh parsley, if desired

Directions:

1. Heat oven to 350 degrees F.
2. Spray 13 x 9" baking dish with cooking spray.
3. Fry bacon until crisp.
4. Drain on paper towels, reserving 2 tbsps. drippings.
5. Crumble bacon; set aside.
6. In large microwavable bowl, stir together mashed potatoes, reserved bacon drippings, the milk, pepper Jack cheese, cream cheese, pepper and 2 cups of the Cheddar cheese.
7. Microwave uncovered on High 4 minutes.
8. Stir in sour cream and chilies until well blended.
9. Spoon potato mixture into baking dish.
10. Sprinkle with bacon and remaining 1 cup Cheddar cheese.
11. Spoon pork evenly over cheese.
12. Drizzle barbecue sauce over pork.
13. Bake uncovered 45 minutes or until bubbly.
14. Let stand 10 minutes before serving.
15. Garnish with parsley.
16. Serve and enjoy!

Spinach Casserole

Ingredients:

1 (16 oz.) package cottage cheese
6 eggs
1/2 cup all-purpose flour
1/4 cup sour cream
2 tsps. salt
1/2 tsp. ground black pepper
2 (10 oz.) packages frozen chopped spinach, thawed and drained
4 cups shredded Cheddar cheese, divided

Directions:

1. Preheat an oven to 350 degrees F.
2. Lightly grease a 9 x 13" baking dish.
3. Place cottage cheese, eggs, flour, sour cream, salt, and pepper in a food processor.
4. Process until smooth.
5. Mix spinach, cottage cheese mixture, and 2 cups of Cheddar cheese in a bowl, then spread into the prepared baking dish.
6. Bake until a knife inserted into the center comes out clean, about 45 minutes.
7. Top with the remaining 2 cups of Cheddar cheese and continue baking until cheese has melted, about 10 minutes.

Potato and Egg Casserole

Ingredients:

6 potatoes
8 eggs
Seasoning salt to taste
1 cup margarine
1 (16 oz.) container sour cream

Directions:

1. Preheat oven to 350 degrees F (175 degrees C).
2. Bring a large pot of salted water to a boil.
3. Add potatoes and cook until tender but still firm, about 15 minutes.
4. Drain, cool, peel and slice.
5. Place eggs in a saucepan and cover with cold water.
6. Bring water to a boil and immediately remove from heat.
7. Cover and let eggs stand in hot water for 10 to 12 minutes.
8. Remove from hot water, cool, peel and slice.
9. In a 9x13 inch casserole dish layer potatoes and eggs, sprinkling each layer of eggs with seasoning salt, ending with potatoes.
10. In a small saucepan over low heat, melt margarine with sour cream.
11. Pour over potatoes and sprinkle lightly with seasoning salt.
12. Bake in preheated oven for 30 minutes.

Green Chile Egg Casserole

Ingredients:

1/2 cup butter
1 (16 oz.) package cottage cheese
1 lb. shredded Monterey Jack cheese
2 (4 oz.) cans diced green chiles
10 eggs
1/4 cup all-purpose flour
1 tsp. baking powder
1/2 tsp. salt

Directions:

1. Preheat oven to 400 degrees F (200 degrees C).
2. Set butter in a 6x10-inch casserole dish.
3. Place dish in the preheating oven until butter is melted.
4. Mix cottage cheese, Jack cheese, green chiles, eggs, flour, baking powder, and salt in a large bowl using an electric hand mixer.
5. Pour mixture into the melted butter in the casserole dish.
6. Bake for 15 minutes. Reduce heat to 350 degrees F (175 degrees C).
7. Bake until middle of casserole is set, about 50 more minutes.
8. Allow to stand for 10 minutes before serving.

Sausage Egg Casserole

Ingredients:

3/4 lb. ground pork sausage
1 tbsp. butter
4 green onions, chopped
1/2 lb. fresh mushrooms, sliced
10 eggs, beaten
1 (16 oz.) container low-fat cottage cheese
1 lb. Monterey Jack cheese, shredded
2 (4 oz.) cans diced green chile peppers, drained
1 cup all-purpose flour
1 tsp. baking powder
1/2 tsp. salt
1/3 cup butter, melted

Directions:

1. Place sausage in a large, deep skillet.
2. Cook over medium-high heat until evenly brown.
3. Drain, and set aside. Melt butter in skillet, and cook and stir the green onions and mushrooms until tender.
4. In a large bowl, mix the eggs, cottage cheese, Monterey Jack cheese, and chiles.
5. Stir in the sausage, green onions, and mushrooms.
6. Cover, and refrigerate overnight.
7. Preheat oven to 350 degrees F (175 degrees C).
8. Lightly grease a 9x13 inch baking dish.
9. In a bowl, sift together the flour, baking powder, and salt.
10. Blend in the melted butter.
11. Stir the flour mixture into the egg mixture.
12. Pour into the prepared baking dish.
13. Bake 40 to 50 minutes in the preheated oven, or until lightly brown. Let stand 10 minutes before serving.

Spinach and Mushroom Egg Casserole

Ingredients:

1 tsp. butter 10 eggs
1 (16 oz.) package cottage cheese
1 (16 oz.) package shredded Monterey Jack cheese
1/2 cup butter, melted
1/2 cup all-purpose flour
1 (10 oz.) package frozen chopped spinach, thawed, drained and squeezed dry
2 (4.5 oz.) cans sliced mushrooms, drained
1 tsp. baking powder
1/2 tsp. salt

Directions:

1. Preheat oven to 350 degrees F (175 degrees C).
2. Grease a 9x13-inch baking dish with 1 tsp. butter.
3. Whisk eggs in a large bowl.
4. Add cottage cheese, Monterey Jack cheese, 1/2 cup melted butter, flour, spinach, mushrooms, baking powder, and salt; mix.
5. Pour egg mixture into prepared baking dish.
6. Bake until eggs are set and a knife inserted into the center comes out clean, about 35 minutes.

Raisin Bread French Toast Casserole

Ingredients:

5 cups cubed cinnamon raisin bread
1 1/2 cups milk
4 eggs
1/4 cup white sugar
1 tsp. vanilla extract
3 tbsps. softened butter, cut into chunks
2 tsps. ground cinnamon

Directions:

1. Preheat oven to 350 degrees F (175 degrees C).
2. Lightly butter an 8x8-inch baking pan.
3. Pour bread cubes into the prepared pan.
4. Beat milk, eggs, sugar, and vanilla extract together in a bowl until evenly mixed.
5. Pour mixture over bread cubes. Arrange butter chunks atop bread mixture.
6. Set aside for bread to absorb liquid, about 10 minutes.
7. Sprinkle with cinnamon.
8. Bake until top is golden, 45 to 50 minutes.

Pear and Almond French Toast Casserole

Ingredients:

1/4 cup butter, cut into
1/4-inch cubes
1/2 cup brown sugar
1 (29 oz.) can pear halves, cut lengthwise into 4 slices
1 (1 lb.) loaf sourdough bread, cut into 1-inch cubes
2 1/2 cups eggs
1 1/2 cups milk
2 tbsps. white sugar
1 tsp. vanilla extract
1/2 tsp. almond extract
1/4 cup sliced almonds

Directions:

1. Evenly distribute the butter cubes into the bottom of a 10x14-inch baking dish.
2. Sprinkle the brown sugar over the butter.
3. Arrange the pear slices into the bottom of the dish. Arrange the bread cubes into a single layer over the pears.
4. Mix the eggs, milk, sugar, vanilla extract, and almond extract together in a bowl until fully blended; pour evenly over the bread cubes, assuring all pieces are evenly covered.
5. Cover the dish with aluminum foil and chill overnight in refrigerator.
6. Preheat an oven to 350 degrees F (175 degrees C).
7. Remove the casserole from the refrigerator and allow to warm while the oven preheats.
8. Bake until the top of the bread is golden brown and the eggs have solidified, 45 to 60 minutes.
9. Top with the sliced almonds to serve.

Blueberry French Toast Casserole

Ingredients:

1 (8 oz.) package cream cheese, softened
1 cup confectioners' sugar
2 tbsps. milk
1 tbsp. vanilla extract, divided
2 cups blueberries, divided
2 loaves French bread, cubed
2 cups milk
8 eggs
1 tsp. ground cinnamon
1/2 tsp. ground nutmeg

Directions:

1. Mix cream cheese, confectioners' sugar, 2 tbsp. milk, and 1 tsp. vanilla extract in a bowl until smooth and creamy; fold in 1 cup blueberries.
2. Cover the bottom of a 10x14-inch baking dish with 1 layer bread cubes.
3. Spread cream cheese mixture over bread layer; top with remaining bread cubes.
4. Whisk 2 cups milk, eggs, 2 tsps. vanilla extract, cinnamon, and nutmeg together in a large bowl; pour over bread mixture. Sprinkle 1 cup blueberries over bread-egg mixture.
5. Cover dish tightly with aluminum foil and refrigerate, 8 hours to overnight.
6. Remove from refrigerator 30 to 60 minutes before baking.
7. Preheat oven to 375 degrees F (190 degrees C).
8. Bake for 45 minutes.
9. Remove foil and continue baking until center is set, about 30 minutes.

Mexican Turkey Corn Bread Casserole

Ingredients:

1 tbsp. canola oil
1 lb. ground turkey
1/4 cup fat-free chicken broth
1 tbsp. taco seasoning mix
2 oz. orzo pasta
1 (8 oz.) jar salsa, or to taste
1 (8.5 oz.) package dry corn muffin mix
1 (8.25 oz.) can cream-style corn
1 tbsp. milk
1 cup shredded Mexican cheese blend

Directions:

1. Preheat oven to 350 degrees F (175 degrees C).
2. Heat oil in a large saucepan over medium-high heat; cook and stir ground turkey in hot oil until turkey is browned and crumbly, 5 to 10 minutes.
3. Drain excess fat.
4. Stir chicken broth and taco seasoning mix into turkey; cook and stir until liquid reduces and thickens, 3 to 5 minutes.
5. Stir orzo into turkey mixture, bring to a simmer, and cook until slightly softened, about 2 minutes.
6. Add salsa to turkey-orzo mixture, stir, and transfer mixture to a 2-quart casserole dish.
7. Stir muffin mix, creamed corn, and milk together in a bowl.
8. Spread corn mixture over turkey mixture.
9. Bake until a toothpick inserted into the center of the casserole comes out clean, 35 to 40 minutes.
10. Spread Mexican cheese blend over the top of the casserole and bake until cheese melts, about 5 minutes.

Turkey and Hash Brown Casserole

Ingredients:

1/4 cup oil for frying
1 lb. frozen hash brown potatoes, thawed
1 lb. ground turkey breast
1 large onion, cut into chunks
1 (10 oz.) package frozen broccoli, thawed
1 (10.75 oz.) can reduced fat cream of mushroom soup
1 cup reduced fat cream of celery soup
1 cup shredded fat free Cheddar cheese
1/3 cup skim milk
1/2 tsp. garlic powder
1/4 tsp. ground black pepper
Seasoned salt to taste
1 medium tomato, diced

Directions:

1. Preheat oven to 400 degrees F (200 degrees C).
2. Lightly grease an 8x12 inch casserole dish.
3. Heat oil in a skillet over medium heat and cook hash browns until golden.
4. Spread hash browns over bottom and sides of casserole dish to form a crust.
5. In a separate skillet over medium heat, cook turkey until lightly brown. Mix in onion and cook until tender. Place broccoli in a microwave safe bowl and cook in microwave 4 to 5 minutes on High, or until tender. Spread turkey, onion and broccoli over hash browns in the casserole dish.
6. In a bowl, mix cream of mushroom soup, cream of celery soup, Cheddar cheese, milk, garlic powder, pepper and seasoned salt.
7. Pour over casserole.
8. Bake 25 minutes, until bubbly.
9. Garnish with chopped tomatoes to serve.

Turkey Butternut Squash Casserole

Ingredients:

1 tbsp. olive oil
1 lb. lean ground turkey
2 cups cubed butternut squash
1 onion, chopped
1 cup milk
1 cup shredded mozzarella cheese
1/4 cup butter, melted
2 eggs
1/2 tsp. salt
1/4 tsp. ground black pepper
1 cup crushed buttery round crackers

Directions:

1. Preheat oven to 375 degrees F (190 degrees C).
2. Grease a 9-inch square baking dish.
3. Heat olive oil in a skillet over medium heat; cook and stir ground turkey until crumbly and browned, 5 to 10 minutes.
4. Add butternut squash and onion to ground turkey; cook and stir until squash is slightly tender, 5 to 10 minutes. Drain any excess grease from skillet.
5. Whisk milk, mozzarella cheese, butter, eggs, salt, and pepper together in a bowl.
6. Stir into turkey mixture.
7. Transfer squash-turkey mixture to the prepared baking dish.
8. Sprinkle crackers over squash-turkey mixture.
9. Bake until cooked through and bubbling, 25 to 30 minutes.

Pancake and bacon Casserole

Ingredients:

2 cups baking mix
2 cups shredded Cheddar cheese, divided
1 cup milk
5 tbsps. maple syrup
2 eggs
1 1/2 tbsps. white sugar
12 slices cooked bacon, crumbled

Directions:

1. Preheat oven to 350 degrees F (175 degrees C).
2. Grease a 9x13-inch baking pan.
3. Mix baking mix, 1 cup Cheddar cheese, milk, maple syrup, eggs, and sugar together in a bowl.
4. Pour into prepared pan.
5. Bake in the preheated oven until a toothpick inserted in the center comes out clean, 20 to 25 minutes.
6. Sprinkle bacon and remaining 1 cup Cheddar cheese over casserole. Return to oven until cheese is melted, about 5 more minutes.

Pancake and Sausage Casserole

Ingredients:

1 (16 oz.) package bulk pork breakfast sausage
4 cups all-purpose flour
1/4 cup white sugar
1/4 cup brown sugar
4 tsps. baking powder
1/2 tsp. salt
4 eggs
2 1/2 cups milk
1/4 cup vegetable oil
1 tsp. vanilla extract

Directions:

1. Preheat oven to 375 degrees F (190 degrees C).
2. Prepare a baking dish with cooking spray.
3. Preheat the baking dish in the oven.
4. Brown the sausage in a skillet over medium heat.
5. Drain.
6. Mix the flour, white sugar, brown sugar, baking powder, and salt in a large bowl.
7. Stir in the eggs, milk, vegetable oil, and vanilla to form a batter.
8. Add the sausage and stir.
9. Pour into the preheated baking dish.
10. Bake until a toothpick inserted into the center of the dish comes out clean, about 25 minutes.
11. Allow to cool 10 minutes before cutting to serve.

Bacon Waffle Casserole

Ingredients:

12 oz. bacon, cooked and cut into 1-inch pieces
8 waffles, freshly made or frozen packaged, quartered
2 tbsps. butter, divided
6 egg yolks
1 1/2 cups buttermilk
1 cup whipping cream
2/3 cup maple syrup, divided
1 tsp. vanilla extract
1/4 tsp. salt
1 1/2 cups mixed fresh berries, such as blueberries, strawberries and blackberries

Directions:

1. Preheat oven to 350 degrees F.
2. Lightly grease 3-quart oven-safe casserole (8 x 10-inch or similar) with 1/2 tbsp. butter.
3. In large bowl, whisk together egg yolks, buttermilk, cream, 1/3 cup syrup, vanilla and salt; reserve.
4. On ungreased rimmed baking pan, spread waffle pieces in even layer and bake for 12-15 minutes or until crisp and lightly toasted.
5. Increase oven temperature to 375 degrees F.
6. Add waffle pieces and bacon to buttermilk mixture and toss to coat evenly.
7. Pour into prepared casserole and tightly cover with foil.
8. Bake for 45-50 minutes and remove foil. Melt remaining butter and brush over top of casserole and bake, uncovered, for another 10-15 minutes or until top is crisp and toasted. Top with fresh berries and remaining maple syrup, dusting with powdered sugar if desired, and serve warm.

Lobster Mac and Cheese Casserole

Ingredients:

2 tsps. vegetable oil
2 lobster tails, split in half lengthwise and deveined
2 tbsps. butter
1 1/2 tbsps. all-purpose flour
1 1/2 cups cold milk
1/4 tsp. paprika
1 pinch ground nutmeg
1 pinch cayenne pepper, or to taste
1/2 tsp. salt, or to taste
3 drops Worcestershire sauce, or to taste
4 oz. grated sharp white Cheddar cheese
1 oz. grated Gruyere cheese
1 cup elbow macaroni, or more to taste
1/2 tsp. fresh thyme leaves
Crumbs:
3 tbsps. panko bread crumbs
1 tbsp. melted butter
2 tbsps. grated Parmesan cheese

Directions:

1. Preheat oven to 400 degrees F (200 degrees C).
2. Butter 2 gratin dishes.
3. Heat oil in a skillet over high heat.
4. Cook lobster tails in skillet until slightly golden and about halfway cooked-through, about 2 minutes per side. Transfer tails to a plate to rest. When cool enough to handle, remove lobster meat from shells and chop meat. Reserve shells.
5. Melt 2 tbsps. butter in the same skillet over medium heat. Whisk in flour.
6. Cook and stir until a paste forms and flour taste cooks off, 1 to 2 minutes.
7. Add cold milk to flour mixture; whisk until completely incorporated.
8. Bring to a simmer; reduce heat to low, and stir in paprika, nutmeg, and cayenne pepper.
9. Cook, stirring occasionally, until thick, 3 to 4 minutes. Season sauce with salt.
10. Stir Cheddar cheese and Gruyere cheese into milk mixture until cheese is melted.
11. Remove from heat and stir Worcestershire sauce into cheese sauce.
12. Bring a large pot of water with reserved lobster tails and a pinch of salt to a boil.
13. Cook elbow macaroni in the boiling water, stirring occasionally, until cooked through but firm to the bite, about 8 minutes. Remove and discard lobster shells, drain pasta.
14. Stir macaroni into cheese sauce with thyme leaves.

15. Divide macaroni mixture between the 2 prepared gratin dishes.
16. Top macaroni with chopped lobster meat, poking meat down into macaroni mixture with a fork.
17. Stir bread crumbs and melted butter together in a bowl.
18. Add Parmesan cheese and stir. Top each gratin dish with bread crumb mixture.
19. Bake in the preheated oven until golden and bubbly, 15 to 20 minutes.

Pumpkin Casserole

Ingredients:

2 cups pumpkin puree
1 cup evaporated milk
1 cup white sugar
1/2 cup self-rising flour
2 eggs
1 tsp. vanilla extract
1/2 cup butter
2 pinches ground cinnamon

Directions:

1. Preheat oven to 350 degrees F (175 degrees C).
2. Combine the pumpkin, evaporated milk, sugar, flour, eggs, vanilla, melted butter and ground cinnamon to taste. Spoon into a casserole dish.
3. Bake at 350 degrees F (175 degrees C) for 1 hour.

Pumpkin Breakfast Casserole

Ingredients:

10 slices white bread, cubed
1 (15 oz.) can pumpkin puree
2/3 cup white sugar
1 tsp. ground cinnamon
1/2 tsp. ground ginger
1/2 tsp. ground nutmeg
1 tsp. vanilla extract
1/8 tsp. salt
6 eggs, beaten
1 cup milk
1 (5 oz.) can evaporated milk
1/2 cup chopped pecans (optional)

Directions:

1. Spray a 9x13-inch baking dish with cooking spray, and place the bread cubes into the dish.
2. In a bowl, mix together the pumpkin puree, sugar, cinnamon, ginger, nutmeg, vanilla extract, salt, eggs, milk, evaporated milk, and pecans.
3. Pour the pumpkin mixture over the bread cubes.
4. Cover the dish with plastic wrap, and refrigerate overnight.
5. The next day, preheat oven to 350 degrees F (175 degrees C).
6. Uncover and bake the casserole until the pumpkin mixture is set and a toothpick inserted into the center of the casserole comes out clean, about 45 minutes.

Cheesy Zucchini Casserole

Ingredients:

4 slices bread, cubed
1/4 cup melted butter
2 cups cubed zucchini
1 large onion, chopped
1 tsp. garlic salt
1 egg, beaten
2 cups shredded Cheddar cheese

Directions:

1. Preheat oven to 350 degrees F (175 degrees C).
2. Place bread cubes in a medium bowl and pour melted butter over the bread.
3. Add the zucchini, onion, garlic salt and egg.
4. Mix well.
5. Transfer the mixture into a 9x13 inch baking dish and top with the cheese.
6. Bake, covered, in preheated oven for 30 minutes.
7. Then uncover the dish and bake for another 30 minutes.

Cheesy Sausage Zucchini Casserole

Ingredients:

1/2 cup uncooked white rice 1 cup water
1 pound pork sausage
1/4 cup chopped onion
1 cup diced fresh tomato
4 cups cubed zucchini squash
2 (4 oz.) cans sliced mushrooms, drained
1 (8 oz.) package processed cheese food, cubed
1 pinch dried oregano
Salt and pepper to taste

Directions:

1. Combine the rice and water in a small saucepan, and bring to a boil.
2. Reduce heat to low, and simmer for about 20 minutes, or until tender.
3. Remove from heat, and set aside.
4. Preheat the oven to 325 degrees F (165 degrees C).
5. Cook sausage and onion in a large skillet over medium heat, stirring until evenly browned.
6. Drain excess grease.
7. Stir in zucchini and tomatoes, and cook until tender.
8. Stir in rice, mushrooms, and cheese. Season with oregano, salt, and pepper.
9. Spread into a 9x13 inch baking dish, or a 2 quart casserole dish.
10. Bake, uncovered, for 1 hour in the preheated oven, or until lightly browned and bubbly.

About the Author

Laura Sommers is **The Recipe Lady!**

She is the #1 Best Selling Author of over 80 recipe books.

She is a loving wife and mother who lives on a small farm in Baltimore County, Maryland and has a passion for all things domestic especially when it comes to saving money. She has a profitable eBay business and is a couponing addict, avid blogger and YouTuber.

Follow her tips and tricks to learn how to make delicious meals on a budget, save money or to learn the latest life hack!

Visit her blog for even more great recipes and to learn which books are **FREE** for download each week:

http://the-recipe-lady.blogspot.com/

Visit her Amazon Author Page to see her latest books:

amazon.com/author/laurasommers

Laura Sommers is also an Extreme Couponer and Penny Hauler! If you would like to find out how to get things for **FREE** with coupons or how to get things for only a **PENNY**, then visit her couponing blog **Penny Items and Freebies**

http://penny-items-and-freebies.blogspot.com/

Other books by Laura Sommers

- **Recipes For The Lumbersexual**
- **Recipes for the Zombie Apocalypse: Cooking Meals with Shelf Stable Foods**
- **Recipes for the Zombie Apocalypse, Vol. 2: Cooking With Foraged Foods**
- **Egg Recipes for People With Backyard Chickens**

May all of your meals be a banquet
with good friends and good food.

Printed in Poland
by Amazon Fulfillment
Poland Sp. z o.o., Wrocław